# The Playbook
# IMPROV GAMES
### For Performers

The Playbook
IMPROV GAMES
for Performers

Collected and Edited by William Hall

Published 2014
© William Hall and Fratelli Bologna
131 Duncan Street
San Francisco, CA 94110
www.fratellibologna.com

Previous versions published as The San Francisco Bay Area
*Theatresportstm Playbook* edited by William Hall and Paul Killam

ISBN: 978-0-9960142-0-5

Book design and production: Jim Shubin, Book Alchemist
www.bookalchemist.net

The Playbook
# IMPROV GAMES
For Performers

Collected and Edited by
WILLIAM HALL

*This Playbook of Improv Games is dedicated
to all those who improvise:*

*"Brave people able to bear the pain of failure"
—Keith Johnstone*

*...this means you!*

Fratelli Bologna
San Francisco, California

# Table of Contents

# Introduction

*This book is for you.*

This is a book designed for you! The improviser. You are part of a brave growing number of performing artists who thrive on facing the unknown. Walking onto a stage with nothing but your beautiful mind and each other

I've been collecting improv games since I began improvising and started BATS Improv in 1986 in San Francisco. In fact, this collection started in 1987 as a few photocopied pages and has now grown to include over 360 games. It was previously published under the name The BATS Improv Playbook of Challenges and was co-edited by my good friend Paul Killam.

Use this book because it has a large collection of games. You could try a different game every time you play and, assuming each game takes an average of 3 minutes to play, you could improvise for 15 hours without ever repeating a game.

Play as many different games as you can. Some improvisers seem to find games that quickly become their favorites... their 'go-to' games. This book contains lots and lots of games, some that you don't know and some that you might not like. It's up to you to try them out.

Challenge yourself to make them theatre games instead of party games. Satisfying the conditions of the game is fun, but it's not enough for a worthwhile evening in the theatre.

Use this book. Put a copy of this book backstage at your theatre, keep it with you when you play, make notes in it and share it with your group.

Please contact me if you know any performance games that aren't in the book; if games are unclear; if you find more than the book's sixteen typos; if you'd like to order a box of them for your troupe or if you have any questions.

Recently I was backstage at BATS Improv before a performance and noticed one of our players, who has been improvising for years, searching through the book. Facing the unknown takes courage....but having a few games in mind can really help.

*William*

William Hall
william@fratellibologna.com

# Index of Categories

Culture
Endowment
Fill in the Blank
Group
Jump
Justification
Lists
Media
Music
Narrative
Other Bodies, Other Players, Other Team
Physical Restriction
Psyche
Scene without Words
Solo Scenes
Status
Technical Zero
Timed
Tossup
Use the Audience
Various Categories
Verbal Restriction

# Games Indexed by Category

The games are listed in the book alphabetically, but we've included this listing by category. Placing games in categories is not an exact science and some of the games are listed in more than one category.

We often find in Theatresports™ that one team will challenge the other team to a category of scenes instead of a specific scene.

*This bold and italic font is for quotes about improv that I like. They remind me of the possibility of improv. They come from the notes I took attending workshops by Keith Johnstone from 1988 to 2011. They do not refer specifically to the games they appear near.*

# The Games
## Listed Alphabetically

The games are listed by the names we know in San Francisco. The descriptions are short by design. This is not a training book of games, it is a reminder of the performance games we play.

Storytelling is the basis of theatre. Some games promote story and others are more useful for variety.

### Key to Game Notes

*(Narrative)* means that the game generally promotes storytelling. *(Filler)* means that the game generally is anti-storytelling. *(Filler/Narrative)* means that the game can go either way.

(K*) means that Keith Johnstone has a comment about the game *(p. 66)*

Category of the game is in italics following the description.

**Accent Roller Coaster.** Players start with a neutral scene. When the emcee/host hits the bell, the Players "freeze" and the emcee/host asks for a new accent (or nationality) from the audience and all the players let that nationality affect them: accent, word use, cultural points of views, etc. Instead of getting suggestions during the scene, the players can get a list of accents before the scene and the emcee/host can call at a new accent whenever he/she "freezes" the scene. *(Filler)* *Verbal Restriction, Lists, Justification*

**Accent Switch.** Players A, B and C each get a different accent from the audience. When the emcee/host "freezes" the scene (or dings a bell), Player A takes on Player B's accent, Player B takes on Player C's, and Player C takes on Player's A accent. emcee/host can freeze again and the next switch occurs. Can also be played with four players (a Player D). *(Filler) Verbal Restriction*

## The Theatresports Motto: Don't Be Prepared.

**Actor Switch.** Scene begins: at some time during the scene an offstage player replaces an onstage character and finishes the scene. The switch may occur when an offstage player freezes the scene, or when an onstage player "freezes". Variation- This can be played with offstage players used as "stunt doubles". **Variation-** An actor is sent out of the room then must replace a character and discover who they are. (See **Understudy**). **Variation-** Other team substitutes for your team (Continuation). (K*) *(Filler) Endowment, Justification*

**Adjective, Scene Based On An.** Players ask for an adjective (for instance, "creepy"), and play the scene illustrating that adjective (with as much 'creepiness' as possible). Or, each player may receive different adjectives. Also may be played as "The Family". *Endowment, Tossup*

**After Hours.** During a scene if a player looks at his/her watch, the time switches to a time yelled out by the audience ("four hours earlier" or "a month later"). (A variation of **Cutting Room**.) See also **Yesterday**. (K*) *(Filler/Narrative) Jump*

**Alien Translator.** An alien visitor has a message for the audience, which another player translates. (a variation of

**Foreign Poet)** *Verbal Restriction, Justification*

> **Keep the risk and danger. The further it gets away from me\*, the more people make it safe. (\*KJ)**

**Alliteration.** Players ask for a letter of the alphabet and incorporate into the scene as many words as possible beginning with that letter. Players may each have a letter. This could be used as a toss-up. (K\*) *(Filler) Verbal Restriction, Tossup*

**Alliteration Die.** Two members from each team stand in a line...a letter is suggested by the audience. When the emcee/host points to a player, they must respond with a word that begins with the suggested letter. The audience yells die if there is an overly long pause or if a player repeats a word. (K\*) *(Filler) Tossup, Verbal Restriction*

**Alliteration sounds**. Each player gets a consonant, and they must speak using only that sound at the beginning of all their words. For example if the players letter was 'P' then instead of saying 'Harrison sit down we need to talk' He/she would say, 'Parrison pit pown pe peed po palk'. *(Filler) Verbal Restriction*

**Alphabet.** The first player's sentence/speech of the scene begins with an "A", the second with a "B", and so on. The final sentence/speech of the scene must begin with a "Z". (K\*) *(Filler/Narrative) Verbal Restriction, Technical Zero*

**Variations: Alphabet in Reverse** (Start with a sentence beginning in "Z", end with sentence starting with the letter "A".)

**Alphabet in Verse.** Sentences rhyme with next sentence of other player.

**Alphabet, Audience Suggestion.** First line begins with the letter suggested by the audience. *(Filler/Narrative) Verbal Restriction*

**Animal Lists.** Two players each get a list of animals. Each player is assigned an offstage partner who during the scene calls out the list of animals at random. The onstage partner must continue the scene using the characteristics of the 'called' animal. *(Filler) Lists, Justification*

**Animal People.** Player (or Players) asks for an animal and plays the scene as a human with that animal's characteristics. (K*) *(Filler) Physical Restriction*

> Keep your challenges as broad as possible.
> Try not to repeat challenges from week to week.

**Arms**. One or more players in the scene have their arms substituted by another player's arms. This can be combined with Experts. This can also be played where audience volunteers supply the arms for the players. (K*) *(Filler) Other Players, Physical Restriction, Use the Audience*

**Asides.** From time to time the players turn to audience and declare their character's true feelings or inner dialogue. The other players maintain a 'soft freeze' (holding still without being rigid) and act as if they have not heard the character's true feelings. (K*) *(Filler) Psyche*

**Attitude Scene.** Players ask for an attitude to have about each other's characters. Can also be an attitude towards a subject or life. (K*) *(Filler/ Narrative) Fill in the Blank*

**Audience, Scene Using**. Players involve all or part of the audience in the scene. May take the form of an Arms Game, Audience as Environment, Moving Bodies, Word-at-a-time Expert, Stop Action Narrative, SoundScape, Teleprompter,

Pillars, Dub Our Musical, Supply the Word, Slide Show, etc. (K\*) *(Filler) Use the Audience, Other Players*

**Authors List.** Players get a list of authors, which the emcee/host writes down. Players start a scene, as they go along the emcee/host freezes the scene and calls out a new author. Can also be played where the new author is solicited from the audience each time the emcee/host freezes the scene. *(Filler) Lists, Justification, Culture*

**Ballet.** The players perform in the style of a ballet. Possibilities include: using a narrator, not using a narrator, and/or taking a familiar story and dancing it. (K\*) *(Filler) Culture*

**Banter.** Players perform a scene and must use a word from the previous sentence of another player. *(Filler/Narrative) Verbal Restriction*

**Bartender.** (Alt names: **It's a Quarter to Two, A Shot And A Song**). Players get a suggestion for a problem. In a Bar, one player sings his problem to the bartender and then the bartender sings the advice or solution. *(Filler) Music*

> **A note on slow motion: Always keep the center of the body moving.**

**Bedtime Story.** A "parent" is telling a "child" a bedtime story that is acted out. The child adds to the story and the acting changes according to what the child says. The 'child' could be an audience volunteer. A variation of Typewriter. (K\*) *(Narrative) Narrative*

**Best *"Blank"*.** Both teams play the same "Best Scene". Anything applies: Current Holiday, Advice from a Parent, or Story. (K\*) *(Narrative) Fill in the Blank*

**Betrayal.** (Also called **Play in Reverse**). The last scene of the play is performed first, the middle scene next and the first scene of the play goes last. The story should be complete (we see all the scenes in the story that lead to that last scene). There need be no actual betrayal in the scene; the name for the game is inspired by Harold Pinter's play of the same name. *(Filler) Psyche, Jump*

**"*Blank*" in a Minute.** An event in a minute. Anything. Birth of a Nation, Epic Movie, Making an omelet, etc. Can be used as a toss-up challenge. (K*) *(Filler) Fill in the Blank, Tossup*

**Blind Freeze Tag**. Similar to Freeze Tag except that the first three players in line have their backs to the scene and the fourth person in line yells the freeze. Can be played as a timed challenge with the freeze called out every 20 seconds or so. *(Filler) Jump, Tossup, Justification*

**Blind Man's Bluff.** Players play a scene either with their eyes closed, or better yet, blindfolded. IMPORTANT SAFETY RULE: Ask the other team to act as "spotters" to keep you on the stage. PLEASE, PLEASE, PLEASE do this. *(Filler) Physical Restriction*

> Keep creating new kinds of challenges and always explore the new ones. Just make sure you can explain them quickly...that is really the only limitation.

**Blind Musical Slips Of Paper.** Slips of paper with phrases or sentences are spread randomly on the floor (or shuffled and divided up among the players). At any time during the scene, players read a slip of paper and use what's written as the first lyric of a short song. The phrases and sentences can be from anywhere. Sources can be: the audience (gather them before the show), random quotes from Shakespeare or lines from Fleetwood Mac's "Rumors", etc. Keep the songs connected to the story of the scene. You are telling a story aren't you? *(Filler) Media, Music, Justification*

**Boris.** Scene in which a player undergoes an interrogation. The player being interrogated is threatened by an invisible thug of gigantic proportion, named Boris. Whenever the interrogator does not get a satisfactory answer, Boris thrashes the prisoner. Emphasize narrative. Remember- the prisoner does not want to be thrashed- the threat inspires the answers. The game is to keep the interrogated person building a satisfying narrative similar to the way New Choice works. *Hint: Remember Keith's advice about falls onstage: "Don't do them."* (K*) *(Filler) Physical Restriction, Narrative*

**Category Die.** Two or more members from each team stand in a line. The audience suggests a category. When the emcee/host points to a player, they must respond with something in the designated category. The audience yells "die" if the named item does not belong to the "category", there is an overly long pause, or if a player repeats a word. If the audience yells, "die", the player is eliminated and then a new category is suggested and the game continues until only one player remains. **Variation: Faux**

**Category Die.** Where players suggest made up things that sound like they belong in that category. *(Filler) Toss-up*

**Chain Murder.** A timed endowments scene. Player A re-mains on stage while the rest of the team is secluded from the stage (often upstage center with their backs to the audience, plugging their ears and closing their eyes). The scene requires three suggestions: an occupation, a room in the house, and an object to be used as a murder weapon.

Using only gibberish, Player A must endow one of his/her teammates ("Player B") with: having that occupation, being in that room, and using that object to kill Player A. Player B repeats the sequence with Player C, and Player C with Player D. With a group of four players, the time limit would be 3 minutes. **Technical Note:** The audience should be requested to applaud when the endowment is done correctly. The emcee/host should quiz the players in reverse order about their occupation, location and weapon. Allow for 1 minute per endowment series. (K*) *(Filler) Endowment, Verbal Restriction, Timed*

**Chain Relationship Endowment.** Instead of an occupation, a room, and a murder weapon...the team asks for: something that might attract you about someone, a location you might go on a date, and a reason to break up. At the end, rather than ending with a murder, each scene ends with a break up. *(Filler) Endowment, Verbal Restriction, Timed*

> **I'd prefer improv to involve the deep subconscious ... I'd rather it weren't a commercial quiz show.**

**Chair.** One chair is placed center stage. One player sits in the chair. Any player, either team, makes an offer which will get the player to get out of the chair. As soon as the chair is empty the player who made the offer sits in it. You cannot block an offer. Players continue to make offers and sit in the chair one after another until the time (a minute) passes and the last player in chair WINS! (**Two Chairs** is a different game!) (K*) *(Filler) Endowment, Timed, Tossup*

**Chance of a Lifetime.** A person is chosen from the audience and questioned about something that they've always wanted to do. The players then stage the event with the audience member.... realizing their Chance of a Lifetime. (K*) *(Filler) Use the Audience*

**Character Traits from the Audience.** The audience provides character traits or character types for the players to use during the scene. It's just that simple. (K*) *(Filler/Narrative) Endowment*

**Clashing Environments**. Players ask for two environments (preferably unrelated). Environments merge during the scene (i.e., Discover America During a Roman Orgy). (K*) *(Filler) Justification*

**Close Up/Long Shot.** When the emcee/host calls out Long Shot, the scene is played with fingers (hands) as the miniature characters in the scene. When the emcee/host calls out Close Up, the scene is played with the players using their whole body. (Variation of Fingers.) (K*) *(Filler/ Narrative) Jump*

**Commercial.** Players ask the audience for a fictitious product. The players then act as a Production Company writing a slogan, jingle and a commercial for that product ... and demonstrate what the product does. (K*) *(Filler) Media*

> It is the risk and struggle between success and failure that makes Theatresports™ work.

**Connect the Lines.** The emcee/host asks for two players from each team (a total of four). The audience gives a first and a last line. One team guesses that they could make a good scene using those lines in 30 seconds. The second team bids a lower time and so on until a team finally does not go lower. If the last team to bid actually does connect the lines in the time they estimated, they win the toss-up. If they go over the time limit or the judges don't think it was a good scene, the other team wins. (A variation of **First Line, Last Line**.) (K*) *(Filler) Tossup*

**Consciences.** Scene where the thoughts of one or more characters are revealed by onstage beings (for instance: angels and devils) or offstage voices. See **Inner Dialogue**. (K*) *(Filler) Psyche*

**Continuation.** Opposing team begins a scene. After 30 seconds the emcee/host dings a bell and the players freeze. The challenging team then assumes the same positions and finishes the scene as the same characters. See **Gradual Continuation**. (K*) *(Filler/Narrative) Group, Justification, Other Team*

**Countdown.** Two-person scene in which players alternate speaking. One player begins by saying a one-word sentence, the other player says a two-word sentence, then three until they get to a ten-word sentence; and then they count back down to a one-word sentence. Conversely, the other player begins with a ten-word sentence and "counts down" to a one-word sentence, then back up to a ten-word sentence. The scene is over when each player has successfully completed the countdown. (See **Step-Word**) *(Filler) Verbal* **Restriction, Technical Zero**

**Creation Myth Scene.** Scene based on the "creation" of something. This could be almost anything, really. How *"Blank"* Was Created. *(Narrative) Narrative*

**Critics.** Two critics introduce the movie. The other players stand by in the wings (this can include the other team). The critics get a movie title from the audience and add a little about the clip they are about to see. The players perform the clip; then the critics introduce a second scene. Ends

after second scene; sometimes after a few scenes. *(Filler)*
*Endowment*

**Cross Talk.** Players provide the voice for each other.
Player A speaks for player B who speaks for player C and so
on. See **Three-Way Dubbing** and **Doublespeak.** *(Filler)*
*Verbal Restriction*

> **I'd rather see scene work, not just a bunch of**
> **actors jumping through hoops; not that I have**
> **anything against jumping through hoops. . .**
> **but not only that.**

**Culture Challenge.** An excuse for an Opera. No, no . . .
seriously, teams do scenes based on "culture"- you know,
Ballet, Shakespeare, Masterpiece Theatre, Musicals,
Performance Art Piece, Beat Poetry, Spoken Word, etc.
Anything that can be seen on Public Television or described
as "cultural". *(Filler/Narrative) Culture*

**Cutting Room.** A player stays out of the scene and acts as a
"film director". The other players begin a scene. At any time
the "film director" may call "cut", ending the scene, and then
may call for a new scene. The new scene can be a jump in
time and/or location. The director may even cut back to the
original scene, call for Close Ups/Long Shots, extreme
Close Ups, establishing shots as well as have DVD extra
scenes, blooper reel, etc. See **Film Rollback.** (K*)
*(Narrative) Jump*

**Da Doo Run Run.** To the tune of the song . . . using a one
syllable name: The first person says, "I met him/her on a
Monday and his/her name was 'Zack'," then EVERYBODY
sings: "Da Doo Run Run Run, Da Doo Run Run," Then the
next person sings the next line, rhyming the first line, "She

had to move so I helped her pack" then EVERYBODY, "Da
Doo Run Run Run, Da Doo Run Run." The next person
does three lines - all rhyming the first line - "Yeah! Her dog
was black, Yeah! It began to attack, Yeah! I scratched its
back" EVERYBODY: "Da Doo Run Run Run, Da Doo Run
Run."... and on and on. Every line rhymes with the first line
until there are no more rhymes. A person is "out" if s/he
pauses, or makes an error in rhyme or scansion. You cannot
use a word that has been used before, even if it has a different
spelling. You cannot mispronounce a word in order to force
a rhyme. You cannot change the end of the word (i.e. add 's'
or 'ed'). *(Filler) Tossup, Verbal Restriction, Music*

> **Don't make it clever, make it worse.**

**Dating Game.** Loosely based on the TV Show of the same
name. Player A is secluded in the sound-proof booth while
the other players get character traits from the audience.
Player A returns and the scene begins. Player A asks
questions of the three prospective 'dates'. Often the same
question is answered by all of them in turn. At the end of a
time limit or question limit Player A is asked which player
they'll choose and why, revealing what character traits he or
she thinks they have. *(Filler) Endowment, Timed*

**Dave's Cards.** This game requires some pre-show preparation. If you are reading this onstage (in front of the
audience) move on to the next game. No one will be the
wiser - unless you are reading aloud, in which case... well...
Make two sets of cards (preferably on two different colors of
card stock). On one set, write instructions. For instance:
"One player onstage must weep uncontrollably..." or: "The
first character to speak must use rhyming couplets..." or: "A
character must confess something shocking..." On the other

set, write conditions. For instance: "...when a bell is rung from offstage." or: "...every thirty seconds." or: "...if they are called by name." Make an effort to see that they work together grammatically. Mix up the cards, and then draw one from each set. Play the rules on the two cards. *(Filler) Justification*

**Day in the Life.** Players ask an audience member for an actual regular day in their life. Players recreate it as they see fit. Also- **Week In The Life-** Scene based on a week in an audience member's date book. Best when timed. The scene could be played as an opera, movie genre or the person's favorite playwright. See also Story from the Audience, Nightmare, What Are You Doing Tomorrow? (K*) *(Narrative) Narrative, Timed*

> **A good idea is one that takes you forward, a bad idea is one that leads you nowhere.**

**Death in a Minute.** Team has 60 seconds to create a scene in which a character dies. It does not matter how quickly or slowly the death happens, as long as it happens in a minute. Death does not need to end the scene. This can be used as a toss-up. Sometimes you must play the full minute. Use your discretion. (K*) *(Filler/Narrative) Timed, Tossup*

**Decreasing Scene.** A short (thirty-second) scene is played normally. The exact scene is played again using three-word sentences, then with no words. *(Filler/Narrative) Timed*

**Delay the Laugh.** (Also called **Laugh'n Go**). Play a scene where the actors must leave the stage when they get a big laugh (not just a few chuckles). They must justify their exit and cannot return to the scene. A variation is that the scene is over when the scene gets a big laugh. When played as a

Tossup, two players from each team play a scene where they all know each other and are all on stage at the same time. When a player gets a laugh from the audience that player must make an excuse to exit the scene. The last actor on stage wins the points or the "toss". The judges may overrule the outcome if a player has not participated fully in the scene (no hiding quietly in the back). The scene can be "honked" if it is boring. (Note: This is a Keith Johnstone game we learned from Dennis Cahill.) (K*) *(Filler) Tossup, Group*

**Different Story, Story Die.** Each person has his or her own story. Or each person has his or her own genre. See **Story, Story, Die**. *(Filler) Tossup, Group*

**Ding & Sing.** Players create a scene and whenever the bell rings (emcee/ host, team member or audience member) the players must break out in song. Similar to **Song Cue** *(Filler) Music*

**Ding Characters.** Characters begin a scene in a neutral style. When the bell rings, each character changes character traits while playing the same scene. Similar in style to Genre List except that the players choose the characters in the instant the bell rings. *(Filler) Justification.*

**Dissociated Images or Words.** A toss-up challenge. Teams are challenged to list as many dissociated images or words as they can in 20 seconds (or other time limit). The audience can judge if they are truly dissociated images. The team with the most wins. Can also be a one-on- one with two players throwing dissociated images back and forth until one of them says an associated image. *(Filler) Tossup, Verbal Restriction*

> **We live between the two, death and sex - we live somewhere between.**

**Distance Game:** Two to three players are in this scene. While other player(s) are in the sound-proof booth, the first player gets a "distance" from the audience. This is the distance they need to maintain from any player that they speak to (e.g. 5 inches or 12 feet). Also called **Go The Distance.** *(Filler) Physical Restriction, Justification*

**Documentary.** A scene played in Documentary style with a narrator. *(Filler/Narrative) Culture*

**Double Endowment.** (Alt names: Secret Environment Endowment, Do This.) Players get a location for the scene to take place. The players in turn enter the sound-proof booth (e.g. they face upstage and plug their ears). Player A asks audience for an activity that he or she must get Player B to do; B does the same for Player A (i.e., if the environment is a hospital waiting room, Player A needs to get Player B to Pray and Player B needs to get Player A to sing.) Usually a three-minute timed scene. *(Filler) Endowment, Timed.*

**Double First Line, Last Line.** Same as **First Line, Last Line** except with two players, who each get a first line and a last line. The scene ends when both players have said their last lines. See First Line, Last Line *(Filler) Fill in the Blank, Technical Zero, Verbal Restriction*

**Double-Doublespeak.** A two-person scene in which player A provides the voice for player B, and vice versa. Consider this **Two-Way Dubbing**. See **Three-Way Dubbing** and **Cross-Talk**. *(Filler) Verbal Restriction*

**Doublespeak.** One player onstage speaks for all the other players in the scene, also for themselves. (A & B start scene-A speaks for A & B. C enters and A speaks for A, B & C, etc.) As a two-person scene, can be played as a **Master/Servant** scene. (K*) *(Filler) Verbal Restriction*

**Driver's License.** Each player asks for a driver's license (or other form of photo ID) from the audience. Players assume the facial expression from the license and play the scene. Hint: Carry the license with you and look at it frequently to remind yourself of the expression. **Variation:** The emcee/host /host may ask the players to switch licenses. *(Filler) Physical Restriction, Endowment*

**Dub our Musical** or **Musical Dub.** One team "acts out" a musical while the other team dubs the songs (using microphones). A very cooperative challenge. Variation: An audience member is in the scene and a player dubs their music. (K\*) *(Filler) Verbal Restriction, Other Players, Music*

**Dubbed Internal Narrative.** Player off-stage dubs for the internal narrative of a (or all) character(s) on stage. See also **Internal Narrative.** *(Filler) Verbal Restriction, Narrative*

> **The audience wants to see what's already there developed. Why add other characters or elements? The tendency is to not trust the present and avoid the future.**

**Dubbing.** Offstage players provide the voices for onstage players. Often done as a **Foreign Film.** See **Three-Way Dubbing, Cross-Talk** and **Subtitles.** (K\*) *(Filler) Verbal Restriction*

**Emcee, Scene Using.** Teams play a scene and must use the emcee/host during the scene, either as a character or a prop, etc. *(Narrative) Other Players*

**Emotional Body Parts.** Players ask for a part of the body and an emotion; then play the scene with that body part having the emotion. *(Filler) Endowment, Physical Restriction*

**Emotional Growing-and-Shrinking Machine**. Each player is assigned an emotion by the audience. As the machine grows, the scene takes on the entering player's emotion. When a player leaves, the emotion of the scene and the scene being played goes back to the earlier emotion and scene. See **Growing-and-Shrinking Machine.** *(Filler)* *Jump, Justification*

**Emotional Party**. Each person gets an emotion. As each enters the party, the party becomes that emotion. As they leave, it goes back to the previous emotion. (Similar to Hitchhiker.) People can enter and leave more than once. (Can be played with people being changed instantly, or more subtly, or with everyone hiding their emotion.) *(Filler/Narrative) Justification*

> **About interacting in a scene: either consummate or break up, either get eaten or make friends, either go together or go apart.**

**Emotional Roller Coaster.** Also known as **Emotional List.** Ask the audience for a list of emotions. One player from the challenging team writes them down and as the scene progresses, that player calls out the emotions from the list. The players assume the emotion, continuing the scene and justifying the rapid changes in emotion. *(Filler) Lists, Justification*

**Emotional Transfer.** Two players start out with different emotions, and gradually change (transfer) to the other player's condition. A time limit may be in order for this scene. (K*) *(Filler) Justification, Timed*

**Ending in "Blank".** Scene must end with a specific phrase or event or activity. (K*) *(Filler/Narrative) Fill in the Blank*

**Endowments.** Endowment scenes are scenes in which one or more players are isolated (go into a soundproof booth), the rest of the team gets secret information from the audience, and when the player(s) reenter, the team tries to share that information with them during the scene without coming out and telling them, thus "endowing" them with the information. The audience applauds a correct endowment. This information is usually activities or attributes, but almost anything is possible. Usually performed with a time limit, the scenes are fast paced and high energy. The teammates do not "show" the player what to do, nor do they play charades or hint or manipulate . . .at least not at first. Create new games with or without time limits and with or without gibberish. See: **Chain Murder, Five Things, Hidden-Word Environment, Murder Endowment, Secret Endowment, Secret-Word Endowment, Environment Endowment,** and **Expert Endowments.** *(Filler) Endowment, Timed*

**English/Gibberish Song.** The players sing a song: when a bell sounds (or other appropriate noise maker), the players switch from normal speech to gibberish. They switch back and forth with every sound of a bell. See also . *(Filler) Music, Verbal Restriction*

**English/Gibberish Switch.** Players play a scene; when a bell sounds (or other appropriate noise maker), the players switch from normal speech to gibberish. They switch back and forth with every sound of a bell. *(Filler) Verbal Restriction*

**Entirely in the Audience, Scene.** The players play the scene entirely while in the audience area. Sometimes, the house lights are turned up and the stage lights are turned down. *(Filler) Use the Audience, Physical Restriction*

> **About starting scenes: If it's horror, start sweet; if it's a love scene, never start as lovers; if it's a murder, start with two little old ladies having tea.**

**Environment Endowment.** Audience suggests an environment, three team members turn upstage and plug their ears, and the fourth gets suggestions of three activities that are performed in that environment. The three players turn around, and over the course of a 3-minute scene, the fourth teammate must endow the others with performing the three activities. Try to avoid making it simply a guessing game. *(Filler) Endowment, Timed*

**Environment Freeze.** Begin with an environment from the audience. Scene begins randomly; the emcee/host or other player freezes the scene, releases some of the players (they leave the playing area) and gives the remaining players a new environment. The players begin a new scene with new characters in that environment while at the same time justifying the positions they are in. All other players join them in the new scene once it is established, then the emcee/host freezes the scene, releases some of the players and gives the remaining players a new environment, and the pattern repeats. The emcee/host may or may not get all environments from the audience. *(Filler) Jump, Justification*

**Environment in a Minute.** Players create as complete an environment as possible in one minute. They can add anything, off-stage sounds, space objects, dialogue and more. This can be used as a toss-up challenge. *(Filler) Timed, Tossup*

**Expert Endowments.** One player is isolated in the soundproof booth. Another player asks for an unusual subject, often by combining two types of suggestions, for example: a mode of transportation and a vegetable (e.g., a man who makes broccoli buses). The second player then interviews the first player, who tries to figure out the unusual subject s/he is an expert on from the hints in the interviewer's questions. *(Filler) Endowment*

> **Performer anxiety kills and inhibits narrative.**

**Experts.** Scene in which at least one player is an expert on a specific subject- real or unreal. Talk shows, lectures, debates and interviews are possible variations. *(Filler) Endowment*

**Eye Contact.** Players make eye contact when music is playing and have no eye contact when music is not playing. Players must justify the eye contact or lack of eye contact. *(Narrative) Physical Restriction, Justification*

**Fairy Tale.** Teams may either improvise an existing fairy tale or improvise their own new fairy tale. Time limits may be imposed. *(Narrative) Culture, Narrative*

**Fairy Tale in A Minute.** Create a new fairy tale based on an audience suggestion in 60 seconds. *(Filler/Narrative) Culture, Timed*

**Family Dinner.** Ask an audience member to help you recreate a typical family dinner from their youth. The players are assigned to play the audience member and other family members. Provide the audience member with a bell and a buzzer. The audience member rings the bell whenever the players get the scene right and the buzzer is sounded when the players miss the mark. **Variations:** First Date or First Day on The Job. Related to **New Choice.** *(Filler) Use the Audience, Group*

**Film Rollback.** Scene begins. At some point, the scene is stopped and returned to a designated event. (Perhaps at the sound of a bell and the call from the emcee/host.) The scene then proceeds in a different direction from that point. Similar to **Cutting Room** and **New Choice.** (K*) *(Filler/ Narrative) Jump*

**Fingers.** Players use fingers as little people and they do the scene as "puppeteers". This may require a bench or some sort of raised platform so the audience can watch the action. See **Close Up/Long Shot.** (K*) *(Filler/Narrative) Physical Restriction*

**First Line, Last Line.** Players receive a first line of dialogue, and an unrelated last line of dialogue. Scene begins and ends with these lines. See **Double First Line, Last Line** and **Connect the Lines.** *(Narrative) Fill in the Blank, Technical Zero, Verbal Restriction*

**Fish Out Of Water.** Two players on a team switch places with the lighting improviser and the musical improviser. The lighting improviser and musical improviser join the team for a scene. *(Filler) Other Players*

> **About judging: if you're throwing "1's", it means you ought to be chucking the scene off the stage long before.**

**Five Things.** Player A leaves the playing area (or enters the sound- proof booth) while his/her partners get five activities from the audience for him/her to do during the scene. "Walk the dog, wash the windows, juggle axes, floss his/her teeth and change a tire." The things should be unrelated to each other. Player A is brought back in and in three minutes his/her teammates must get him/her to do the activities. The team should not tell Player A, show Player A, or use charades to get the Player A to do these activities; the team tries to lead them to each activity, subtly. If the player doesn't "get" the activity, his/her teammates can become bolder, more obvious, and then blatant until Player A DOES each activity. The scene is the most successful if Player A tries to DO anything that crosses his/her mind. Instruct the audience to applaud when the player DOES each correct activity. It helps to have a strong "where". The danger with this challenge is that it becomes a party game: so try to tie the activities into a story. *(Filler) Fill in the Blank, Endowment, Timed*

**Flirting with the Horn.** The players try to be 'almost' boring but not so boring as to actually get a horn-for-boring call (which would end the scene in a Theatresports™ match). *(Filler)*

**Foreign Film.** Players ask for a foreign country or film-maker. The players begin a scene speaking in the gibberish foreign language and are translated by other teammate(s). The translators can be at the front edge of the stage on microphones. Similar to Dubbing. (Also called **Foreign Translator**.) *(Filler) Verbal Restriction*

**Foreign Poet.** The name of a real country is asked for from the audience. Player then introduces a guest poet from that country (e.g. Poet Laureate of Lithuania), who speaks in gibberish with a Lithuanian accent. One player will translate. Can also add an interpretive dance of the poem as the poet is speaking or have an American Sign Language translator. See also **Alien Translator**. *(Filler) Verbal Restriction, Justification*

**Fortune Cookie Challenge.** A fortune cookie is opened and read aloud. The scene must use the fortune in some way (i.e., philosophical basis, event during scene . . . etc.). Each player may open a cookie and base their characters on the fortune. *(Filler) Justification*

**Forward/Backward Opera.** Do a scene in the style of opera and every time the bell is dinged the opera jumps in time forward or reverse. *(Filler) Music, Jump*

**Forward/Reverse.** Players improvise a scene until the emcee/host rings a bell and calls for the scene to move in reverse (rewind). When the bell rings again the scene moves forward and so on. *(Filler) Physical Restriction*

> **Most good narrative involves a moral decision. Do a scene involving a moral decision. You don't have to agree with it, but you do have to make a moral decision.**

**Four-Letter Word.** Players ask for a four-letter word from the audience. This word is used in the first player's sentence. When the next person speaks, his/her sentence has the four-letter word with one letter changed. For example, if the word is "head", the first sentence could be "My **head** hurts". The next player may say, "That's because you **held** it for so long between your knees." The word does not change in every sentence, it changes whenever a new person starts to speak. *(Filler) Verbal Restriction*

**Four Monologues.** Each player tells a brief monologue. The monologues are narratively connected. See also Orlando Monologue. *(Narrative) Narrative, Group*

**Free Association - Reincorporation.** Player free-associates images for 30 seconds providing disconnected phrases and images. Opposing team plays a scene or tells a story based on the free association, using as many of the images as possible.

Again the challenge is to wrap the images into a story not just repeat them. *(Narrative) Justification, Other Players*

**Free Stage.** Timed Challenge. One team challenges the other team to the best use of the stage in a time limit, for example, four minutes. The suggestion getting is included in the time. Teams must do more than one kind of challenge (i.e. you cannot do a four minute musical). *(Narrative) Timed*

**Freeze Tag.** Two players begin a scene. Another player (offstage) calls out "FREEZE"- players onstage freeze and a new player tags out one of the onstage players. New player then assumes the exact physical position of the tagged-out player and starts a new scene by justifying the positions in the new scene. Players "freeze" in and out as often as is desired. See also **Environment Freeze, Blind Freeze Tag, Reality Freeze.** *(Filler) Jump, Tossup, Justification*

> **If you are on stage with no sense of being looked at, the audience will watch you. You can come on blank. Don't be imaginative. Get in trouble.**

**Full Deck.** This status game requires a deck (or several decks) of cards. Players shuffle the deck(s) and divide up the cards. Players then hold their allotment of cards face out on their forehead (without looking at them). Players treat each other as if the card showing represents their status. Every few lines, toss away the top card. (Note- if you are using this game in performance, try to find a deck of oversized cards so the audience can see them.) (Filler) Status

**Funny-Smelly-Sexy.** Each player secretly endows other players with one of these qualities, and then plays a scene (often a party). (Hint: Play the scene real and polite). **Variation: Funny-Intelligent-Dangerous.** See also **Emotional**

**Party** and **Obsession Party.** (K*) *(Filler/Narrative) Endowment*

**Genre House.** Each "room" in a house is given a different film genre; the scene takes place in a house and the actors travel from room to room, changing from genre to genre. *(Filler) Endowment, Physical Restriction*

**Genre Replay.** A short scene is replayed in different genres or styles. (See **Rashomon, Styles**) *(Filler) Lists, Justification*

**Genre Roller Coaster.** The audience provides a list of genres that is written down by the emcee/host or another player. The players begin a scene and from time to time the emcee/host calls out one of the genres from the list and the players continue the scene in the new genre. (Also known as **Genre Lists** and **Genre Switch.**) *(Filler) Lists, Justification*

**Genre Scene.** Play a scene in a genre style (Film Noir, Sci-Fi, Western, Screwball Comedy, Shakespeare, Action, Swashbuckler, etc.) *(Narrative) Culture, Narrative*

> **About the lack of quiet moments: as soon as you think ahead, you speed up. Your mind has gone to the future because you're unsure of yourself.**

**Genre Transfer.** Players must switch gradually from one style of narrative (genre) to another. This can be a timed transfer like **Status Transfer.** *(Filler) Culture, Timed*

**Gibberish Interpreter.** Two players speak in gibberish. Middle player speaks English, translating for both of them. Often some conflict is resolved. See also **Police Interrogator.** *(Filler) Verbal Restriction*

**Gibberish Opera**. An opera is sung in Gibberish. Variation: Gibberish/ English Opera Switch. See also Subtitles. *(Filler)*

*Verbal Restriction, Music, Culture*

**Gibberish Scene.** Any scene played in gibberish (i.e. an imaginary language). (K*) *(Filler/Narrative) Verbal Restriction*

**The Good, the Bad and the Ugly Advice.** Three players provide advice from questions posed by audience members. Start with the Good advice, followed by the Bad advice and ending with the Ugly advice. A different player starts each round of advice. *(Filler)*

**Gradual Continuation.** The opposing team starts a scene and is replaced one at a time by the members of the challenging team by yelling, "freeze". The team member who yells, "freeze" tags out one member of the other team and continues the same scene in the character of the player tagged out. See **Continuation.** *(Filler/Narrative) Other Team, Group, Justification*

## Be brave...you're making it up

**Greater Than, Less Than.** Pecking Order with a verbal twist. Player 1 with the highest status determines how many words the other players can use in their sentences, based on the number of words used in their own sentences. For example, if player 1 said seven words, then player 2 must use six words or less and player 3 must use fewer words than player 2 and so on. As long as the person with lower status *says a shorter sentence than the person ahead of him/her on the pecking order, it's fine.* (Filler) Verbal Restriction, Status

**Growing-and-Shrinking Machine.** One player begins a scene. Player 2 freezes the scene, and starts a new scene. Player 3 freezes that scene and begins a new scene. Player 4 freezes scene, starts a new scene, and finds a reason to leave.

Players 1, 2 & 3 freeze as Player 4 leaves, and the scene reverts back to the third scene. Player 3 finds a reason to leave, Players 1 & 2 freeze, then revert to second scene. Player 2 finds a reason to leave, and Player 1 freezes, then the scene reverts to the original (first) scene. Ta-Da! New body positions are justified throughout the game (in its entirety). Similar to **Space Jump.** See also **Emotional Growing** and **Shrinking Machine, Shrinking & Growing Machine.** *(Filler/ Narrative) Jump, Justification*

**Guardian Angel.** Players get an audience member to be their guardian angel. The Audience member walks around the stage with the player and occasionally taps the player on the shoulder when they have something they want the player to say, and conversely when the player is stuck for words, they can tap the guardian angel on the shoulder to supply the dialogue. Can also be played with the audience member as the character and the player as the "Guardian Angel". *(Filler) Use the Audience*

**Half Life.** A scene is played in 60 seconds then repeated in 30 seconds then again in 15 seconds and again in 7.5 seconds and then again in 3.75…. and, maybe, again in …well, you get the idea. *(Filler) Timed*

**Variation: Double Life:** A 7.5 second scene is played, then repeated in 15 seconds and again in 30 seconds and finally in 60 seconds. *(Filler) Timed*

**Happily Ever After.** A team gets the suggestion of a well-known fairy tale and they improvise the story after the well-known Happily-ever-after ending…. to see what happened next. **(Narrative) Culture, Narrative**

**Hat Game.** Two players from opposing teams put on hats of approximately equal dimension (ideally wide-brimmed models) and play a scene. Scene ends when a player grabs the hat off the opponent's head or a player grabs for the hat and misses. Take the hat off if you wish but keep the hat at risk as much as possible. Play the scene for its own value. The judges or emcee/host may reward good Theatresportsmanship and risk-taking. (K*) *(Filler) Tossup*

**He Said, She Said.** Game where players describe the actions of their partners onstage. Example: Player 1 says: "I'd like to talk to you, Mabel." Player 2: "He said" (referring to Player 1), "standing up and putting his hands on his hips." Player 2 continues, "All right." 1: "She said," (referring to Player 2) "pulling out her bullwhip and snapping it over my head." Etc. Players must freeze in position until other players describe their action. This can also be played with two players offstage calling the actions. Player 1 says, "I'd like to talk to you, Mabel." Player 3 says from offstage, "He said, standing up and putting his hands on his hips." (K*) *(Filler/Narrative) Verbal Restriction*

> **Good improvisers are experts at being on stage looking like they're not performing.**

**Hidden Word Environment.** All members of the team leave, the emcee/ host asks the audience for an environment and for three words which might be used in that place. When the team re-enters, they are given only the environment and they begin a scene while trying to discover the three words. The audience is coached to respond to the teams to let them know when they're are getting "warmer", i.e. when the team begins an activity which might lead to the word, the audience may "Ohh!"; if the team continues the audience may call out "Aah!" and when the team says the word the audience cheers. *(Filler) Endowment, Timed*

**The Hitchhiker Game.** One player is driving in a car and picks up a hitchhiker with some kind of quirk (a broad Scottish burr, or hiccoughs, or a tendency to burst into song - that sort of thing). When the hitchhiker gets in the car, the neutral driver takes on that quirk. Each time a new passenger is added, all of the travelers take on the new quirk. *(Filler) Justification*

**Humans, Scene Without.** Scene in which no players may play humans. *(Filler) Physical Restriction*

**I Love You Scene.** Usually serious. "I love you" is subtext (mantra) for each player during the scene and is never spoken. (Often played with only two players.) (K*) *(Narrative), Verbal Restriction, Psyche*

**The Impossible Scene.** Ask the audience for an activity to start the scene. All the players must be involved in the activity and continue the scene without "I", "me" or "my"... also no questions... and you cannot refer to the activity. Tough enough for ya? *(Filler) Verbal Restriction, Technical Zero, Tossup*

**In and Out.** Each player gets a word from the audience. During the course of the scene, if the word is used, the player must either enter or exit the scene, depending on whether the player is offstage or on. Players may not use their own word. (Or so we have been told.) You can ask for a genre and get words that would be part of that genre e.g. Shakespeare ("forsooth", "anon") or western ("howdy", "wrangler"). *(Filler) Verbal Restriction, Physical Restriction*

**Inner Dance-a-Logue.** Like Inner Song-a-Logue but with interpretive dance as self-expression rather than a song or monologue. The emcee/ host can call out a player's name to "trigger" the dance. *(Filler) Psyche*

Most audiences will train improvisers to gag and kill narrative by laughing at gags. You can hear a laugh or giggle but you can't hear a tear fall.

**Inner Dialogue.** Players perform a scene and have offstage "voices" create the inner dialogue for them. Sometimes played with just one character having an Inner Dialogue. See **Consciences.** *(Filler) Psyche*

**Inner Song-a-Logue.** Similar to a musical, except that the songs are inner monologues and therefore not heard by other characters. It helps to think that your character is so filled with emotion, that only a song will express your feelings. The emcee/musician can call out a player's name to "trigger" the song. Note. **"Song Cue"** is a different game where the song is heard by other characters. *(Narrative) Music, Psyche*

**Innuendo.** Players flirt with the bag, making as many innuendoes, double-entendres or suggestive remarks as possible. This can be a one-on-one, with tag-outs, or a straight scene. If you get bagged, you lose. *(Filler) Verbal Restriction*

**Interference.** Team begins a scene. Opposing team attempts to take focus without speaking, making noise, or touching the opposing team members. This can be played as the most successful interference wins, or the successful scene wins. *(Filler) Justification, Other Team*

**Internal Narrative.** Scene in which one player tells a story, usually in the first person (i.e., "I went down to the docks . . .") while the rest of the team interacts with her/him, providing environment and supporting characters. You can have either one internal narrator throughout the story or others may have their own narration. See also **Dubbed Internal Narrative.** *(Narrative) Narrative*

**Invent-a-Game.** (Sometimes called **Research & Development** and **On the Spot.**) A player asks the audience for a phrase or word. The player then invents a game based on that suggestion. Hint: Make it up as quickly as possible; trying to make it clever or "good" will almost always backfire. *(Filler) Fill in the Blank*

**Invisibility Scene**. One or more characters in the scene are invisible. The invisible characters can be an off-stage voice, physically on-stage but invisible to all players or physically on stage and visible to one player but not to others. Or any other variation you can think of. (K*) *(Filler) Justification*

> **It doesn't have to be perfect, it's the nature of sport.**

**Isn't It Human Nature?** One player stands to the side of the stage. The other players play a scene. When the emcee/host rings a bell, the onstage players freeze and the observing player must make a comment about the scene beginning with the phrase, "isn't it human nature..." And then the scene continues until stopped again. *(Filler/Narrative) Endowment*

**Job Roller Coaster** or **Job Switch**. The emcee/host asks the audience for a list of occupations. The Players play a scene and as the emcee/host calls out the new occupation, the players must play the character with the traits of that occupation. *(Filler) Lists, Justification*

**Judges' Cards.** Each player is assigned a number between "1" and "4". The Judges each hold up a number. Those players play a scene. The emcee/host calls "change", the judges hold up different numbers and the scene changes and those players whose numbers were displayed perform the new scene. This continues until the scene ends itself or a time limit is satisfied. Note: It's okay if more than one judge throws the same number. *(Filler/Narrative) Justification, Timed*

---

**Take deep breaths, avoid shallow breathing.**

---

**Just a Scene.** A scene without any verbal or physical restrictions ... no fillers, no restrictions. *(Narrative) Narrative*

**Justify The Sound.** A team plays a scene while sounds are contributed by the other team or sound improviser, and the team must justify the sounds. A team might bring in noisemakers in preparation for this challenge. See SoundScape. *(Filler) Justification, Other Team*

**Kiddie Show.** A scene done in the style of a children's show. *(Filler) Culture*

**Knife Game.** A two-player scene in an intimate setting; honeymoon or first date. Midway through the scene, one player (or both players) takes out an imaginary knife, plunges it into his/her forehead and cuts down the middle of his/her own face and body and then removes his/her own skin like a suit of clothes to reveal the true self underneath. *(Filler) Psyche*

**Last Letter-First Letter.** Verbal restriction scene. Last letter of Player A's sentence must be first letter of Player B's sentence. Example- B: "I told you to be home early". A: "**Y**es, you did, but I thought you were only joking" B: "**G**uess what? I wasn'**t**." A: "**T**oo bad." May be used as a toss-up. *(Filler) Verbal Restriction, Technical Zero, Toss-up*

**Last Word-First Word**. The last word of a player's speech must be the first word of the next player's speech. *(Filler)* *Verbal Restriction*

**Light Booth Challenge.** Also known as **Booth Hell**. Light operators may do as they please and players must do their best to justify the changes that occur around them. *(Filler)* *Other Bodies, Justification*

**Limerick Musical.** Players sing using the structure of a limerick (A, A, B, B, A) Players can either perform a musical using just songs in limerick form (where each player sings a song) or they can line up center-stage and each player sings a line at a time, going through all the players a number of rounds (or until the song is done). *(Filler) Music*

**Limerick Story.** Players stand in a line downstage and tell a story in the form of limericks (A, A, B, B, A). Each player supplies a line of a limerick and they continue creating limericks until the story is complete. *(Filler/Narrative)* *Group, Toss-up, Verbal Restriction*

**Line.** One actor begins a monologue (from an audience suggestion or not), occasionally calling "line" as if they have forgotten the next line in the monologue. Another player holding an imaginary script "reads" from the script the next line, and the monologue continues using that line. *(Narrative) Fill in the Blank*

**Lists -** Ask the audience for a list...any list...attitudes, body parts, countries, emotions, genres, authors, historical periods, animals, TV shows, playwrights, movie directors, etc. Then play a scene, occasionally freezing, then continuing using the next item on the list. See **Emotional Roller Coaster, Animal Lists, Genre Roller Coaster, TV Channel,**

GAMES    THE PLAYBOOK    *51*

**Author List, Accent Roller Coaster.** *(Filler)* *Lists, Justification*

> **Unless you fail half the time, success doesn't mean anything.**

**Lounge Singer** (alt name: **Cabaret Environment, Try the Veal, Where Are You Folks From?**) The Players get a suggestion of a location and a singer, and then play a scene in that location with a lounge act in the style of the suggested singer. So you may end up in a Dairy Queen with 'Elvis Costello' as the lounge act. *(Filler) Music*

**Love Me Tender.** Before entering the scene, a player calls freeze, waits for the scene to freeze, and then asks the audience whom in the scene (or on the bench) they are in love with. When they enter, the scene continues. See **Love Status and I Love You Scene.** *(Filler) Endowment*

**Love Status.** Before the scene, everyone on stage is assigned another person whom they are in love with. The scene is played out. *(Narrative) Status, Endowment*

**Machine.** Players (one by one) form parts of a machine using body movements and sounds. Machines may represent a real machine, a machine that makes a product, an environment, an emotion, a genre of film, etc., as suggested by the audience. *(Filler) Physical Restriction, Tossup*

**Machine - Scene.** Players create a machine (see **Machine**) and then, as their motions suggest a situation, they gradually work into a scene, justifying their body movements.After a scene they evolve into a new machine. Theemcee/host or challenging team specifies the number of scenes and machines to be performed (**Scene-Machine-**

Scene-Machine- Scene or Machine-Scene-Machine, etc.). *(Filler) Physical Restriction*

**Madrigal.** A musical challenge. Each player asks for a suggestion- phrase, proverb, parental warning, old saying, quotes from the Bible or Shakespeare, advertising slogans, bumper stickers, headlines or lines of dialogue will do. Players then begin to sing their suggestions in madrigal form- (unfortunately, there is not a good, succinct way of explaining "madrigal form"- sorry). Each player should sing their phrase one at a time, establishing their phrase and musical part. After all players join the madrigal, words are traded back and forth, making new phrases out of old, until players feel the madrigal is over, and bring the song to a close. See also **Narrative Madrigal** and **New York Madrigal.** *(Filler) Music, Group*

> **Get your players to investigate misbehavior.**

**Make a Face.** Each player gets an audience member to make a face. The player mimics the face and uses it as the basis of his/her character in the ensuing scene. See also **Driver's License.** *(Filler/Narrative) Justification, Use the Audience, Physical Restriction, Other Bodies*

**Master/Servant Scene.** Scene in which one player is the Master, the other the Servant. Best if the two players are not assigned the role but find out in front of the audience which one they are. Make the scene about the relationship; it really is not a scene about ordering another player around. *(Filler) Status*

**Masterpiece Theatre.** A scene played in the style of Masterpiece Theatre. *(Filler/Narrative) Culture*

**Media Challenge.** Players perform a scene based on some sort of published material: newspaper headlines, tabloid headlines, personal ads, Dear Abby, *TV Guide* synopses, "Ripley's Believe It or Not", *US Magazine*, "Guinness Book of World Records", or other anecdotal publications. The shorter the sources are, the better. *(Filler/Narrative) Media*

**Medley from a Musical.** The players improvise a medley of the songs from a fictitious musical. Each snippet is a short, 10 – 20 seconds, a line or a verse. See also **Mix Tape**. *(Filler) Music, Group*

> **Keep your other players in the audience from making suggestions.**

**Member of the Opposing Team, Scene Using A.** A member of the opposing team takes part in the playing team's scene. The audience may be called upon to select the member of the opposing team who is to take part in the scene. *(Filler/Narrative) Narrative, Other Team*

**Minute-Long Scenes.** A scene that lasts no longer than one minute. Can just perform a scene or try Death in a Minute, Love in a Minute, Epic in a Minute, Movie in a Minute, Fairy Tale in a Minute, Most Justified Exits and Entrances in a Minute, This Show Tonight in a Minute, all sorts of possibilities. *(Filler/Narrative) Timed, Tossup*

**Mix Tape.** Get a topic to make a mix tape about (love, breaking up, growing up, mothers, forgiveness). Sing improvised snippets of songs (a line, a verse) that are about 10-20 seconds long. The mix tape is not from just one musical so there can be a range of musical styles. Similar to **Medley from a Musical.** *(Filler) Music, Group*

**Monosyllabic Scene.** A scene where each word has just one syllable. This could be a plain scene or a Shakespearean Scene. *(Narrative) Verbal Restriction*

**Most Endowments.** A timed scene in which players must endow the scene every time they enter, which is as often as possible. *(Filler) Endowment, Timed, Tossup*

**Most Scenes in A Minute.** Teams perform as many scenes as they can in one minute. Judges score the scenes on their entertainment value. emcee/ host t keeps track of the number of scenes and awards extra points for the team with the most scenes. When used as a toss-up, the scenes are not judged. *(Filler) Timed, Tossup*

**Most Scenes Using an Object.** Players use one (real) object in as many scenes as they can during a specified time period, endowing the object anew with each scene. *(Filler) Endowment, Timed, Tossup*

**Move On.** The emcee/host or member of the team calls out "move on" every so often and the current scene must stop and a new scene must start. The scenes must be part of the same story and move the story forward in time. The new scene often changes location. *(Narrative) Jump*

**Move On Musical.** The players begin a musical; the emcee/ host or a member of the team calls out "move on" every so often a new scene from the musical must start. The scenes must be part of the same story and move the story forward in time. In the "new" scene, players can start with dialogue and then break into song. The new scene often changes location. *(Filler) Jump, Music*

> **On a "bad night", do gibberish scenes or word-at-a-time scenes.**

**Movie Trailer.** One team does three short excerpts from a movie trailer, and the other team does the movie incorporating the trailer scenes. See **Critics.** *(Filler/Narrative) Endowment, Justification, Other Team*

**Moving Bodies.** Audience members or teammates provide the locomotion for players in the scene while players provide the dialogue. Players may not move any part of their bodies on their own. (K*) *(Filler) Other Bodies, Physical Restriction, Use the Audience*

**Multiple Narrators.** The players switch off taking the role of narrator during the scene. *(Narrative) Narrative*

**Multiple People Person.** Two or more players move and speak as one unit. See also **Two-Headed Mutant.** *(Filler/Narrative) Physical Restriction, Verbal Restriction*

**Murder Endowment. (Not Chain Murder.)** Audience selects one player to be a "murderer", who leaves room while remaining team gets suggestion of location, murder weapon and victim. Murderer returns, the scene is played while the team endows the murderer with the information until she/he kills the correct victim with weapon. Usually a three-minute timed scene. *(Filler) Endowment, Timed*

**Music, Scene From.** Musician begins playing; actors begin a scene inspired by mood conjured by music; music fades out. See also: Scene Starting With Interpretive Dance. *(Filler) Justification, Music*

> **Trying to do your best means too much effort! Total terror. Be average, try to have a pleasant and nice time.**

**Music, Scene To.** Players perform a scene to music from the booth or live musician. The musical styles (offers) change during the scene. Players continue the narrative, justifying the new mood. May or may not be a silent scene. It is unnecessary to ask for a suggestion. Music may be played from the beginning of the scene, or may be cued at a point during the scene. *(Filler) Music, Justification*

**Music Video.** Scene performed in the style of a music video. Often performed with one of the players singing the song and others supplying the visual. *(Filler) Music, Endowment*

**Musical.** A scene in the style of a musical. This can be a brief excerpt of a Broadway Musical (also known as **Scene-Song-Scene**), a big closing number, or as an accelerated complete musical (aka **Musical in Three Minutes** or **Move on Musical**). Can also do a Rock Opera, a Bollywood Musical. Or ask for Musical Lyricist or director: Cole Porter, Gilbert & Sullivan, Stephen Sondheim, Baz Lurhmann, Bob Fosse, etc. *(Narrative) Music*

**Musical Hot Spot.** When the musician is playing, you sing. When the musician stops playing, you speak. The other players can hear your song. Perhaps your character is so filled with emotion, that only a song will do! Similar but different are **Inner Song-a-logue** and **Song Cue**. *(Filler) Music*

**Musical Rashomon.** Players perform a short scene. When the end of the scene is reached, the players repeat the scene three times. Each time is influenced by different musical styles provided by the sound or music improviser. See Styles. *(Filler/Narrative) Justification, Music*

**My Very Own Director (Side Coach).** Each player is assigned a director/ coach (two players from a team are the actors and two are the coaches). From time to time, when the emcee/host rings the bell, the scene stops and the players refer to their coaches for advice. When the emcee/host rings the bell again the scene resumes. See **Side Coach Challenge.** *(Narrative.) Group*

**Narrated Story.** A scene that is narrated by a player. Similar to Typewriter, without the typewriter. See Multiple Narrators. *(Narrative) Narrative*

> **Put a sign at your box office that says, "This is not family theatre."**

**Narrative Madrigal.** Similar to a Madrigal challenge except that the 'song' develops into a story. (Hint: repeat the most recent line of narrative.) Also called **New York Madrigal** (except in New York). *(Filler/Narrative) Music, Group*

**Narrative Scene.** An open challenge allowing the players to perform any type of scene with the story as the major focus. **(Narrative) Narrative**

**Narrative Scene Commentary.** Two players sit off stage and provide narrative commentary for the other players throughout the scene. For example: (Commentator, "He's avoiding eye contact, it may mean that he is feeling guilty.") See also **Slow Motion Commentary**. *(Narrative) Narrative*

**New Choice.** An open scene where the emcee/host (or a teammate) occasionally calls out "New Choice". When this happens, the player who last spoke (or offered) must make another choice. Hint: Allow the scene to get started for a while before calling for new choices. New choices that lead to risk-taking are encouraged. Go into the cave! *(Filler)* *Justification*

**New York Madrigal.** Like a madrigal except that the players are telling a story through the song. See **Narrative Madrigal.** *(Filler/Narrative) Music, Group*

**Newspaper Headline.** A scene based on a current headline from the newspaper or tabloid. The headline can be obtained by asking the audience for a page number and a column number. Sometimes called **Media Challenge.** Also see **TV Guide.** *(Filler/Narrative) Media*

**Nightmare.** Similar to **Day in the Life** except that the events of a person's day are played as a nightmare. *(Filler) Psyche, Use the Audience*

**Nine Lines.** A scene that only has nine lines and is repeated with different Attitudes, Points of View or Genres. Three players, three lines each, is a good place to start. *(Filler) Justification*

**No, You Didn't!** Solo Scene. A player starts telling a first person story (it can start out a "true" story). Whenever it seems like there's an embellishment, an unrealistic or unbelievable choice in the story, the audience calls out "No you didn't!" and the player revises the story (which is now, definitely, fiction) and continues. *(Filler) Solo Scene, Justification*

**Non Sequitur.** Players are assigned numbers. When a judge holds up a number, the player must says a non sequitur that the other players must justify. *(Filler/Narrative) Justification*

**Nothing, Scene From.** No suggestion is taken from the audience. Teams perform a scene without planning anything. It is best if the person starting the scene walks onstage with his/her mind a blank and lets inspiration strike at will. Try not to plan or use anything you have seen (or thought of) before. (K*) *(Narrative) Narrative*

**Object Endowment.** A member of your team leaves the stage area (for the "soundproof booth") while the audience assigns objects to the members of the opposing team. Members of the opposing team then assume physical positions suggesting that object. Your teammate is brought back in, and a scene is played in which the teammate tries to use/identify each object. Usually within a time limit. (Filler) *Endowment, Timed*

**Accept any challenge, practice it, get better.**

**Objects from the Audience, Scene Using.** Players perform a scene using an object from the audience. One does not have to use the object as itself. The object could be used as a prop, religious icon, or anything. Also called **Prop Endowment.** *(Filler) Endowment*

**Obsession Party.** Everyone gets an obsession. First do it broad, then again with people hiding their obsessions. You want general obsessions (how things feel, guilt) as opposed to more specific (cars). (Hint: People tend to play obsessions on one level. It is interesting to hide the obsession. Don't make the obsession the focus of the scenes: focus on the narrative.) *(Filler/Narrative) Justification*

**Old Job, New Job.** Two players play a scene involving a profession (a job). The audience suggests what their job was in a 'previous life' and the players must play the new profession but with the influences of the previous job. *(Filler) Justification*

**In Theatresports™ you should challenge to the same game; the audience wants to compare the teams. Don't always challenge to categories. Challenge to games.**

**One Eighty-Five.** (Tossup challenge). A player from each team gets a suggestion from the audience of a noun (a telephone, an airplane pilot, a semi colon). Player A says, "185 s walk into a bar, the bartender says, "I'm sorry but we don't serve s here." Then Player A supplies the punch line. Then Player B does the same thing. They go back and forth like this until one of them can't think of anything or for a specified time limit. Sometime the judges or audience votes on which one 'won' the competition. *(Filler) Tossup*

**One-Hit Wonders.** Many games are primarily "one-timers" and are not as good the second time they are played. The team performing second is usually at a disadvantage (the novelty often wears off). Three or more of these types of scenes (Arms, Moving Bodies, Sideways Scene, Boris, etc.), are written on slips of paper, and drawn from a conveniently available hat. (K*) *(Filler) Various Categories*

**One-Word-at-a-Time Scene.** Similar to **Two-Headed Mutant.** Players get into groups of two (or more) and speak a word-at-a-time as if they are one character. So two players could be the bride and the other two players could be the groom. (K*) *(Narrative) Verbal Restriction*

**One-word Story, Story Die.** Similar to **Story, Story Die**, except that players say only one word-at-a-time when pointed to by the emcee/host. *(Narrative) Group, Tossup*

**One-On-Ones. (High/Low Status, Most (adjective) In a Minute, No Gagging, No Blocking)** One member from each team plays a scene. Players attempt to illustrate the specific suggestion better than their competitor. Don't be limited by this list. Anything goes, holding your breath, most push-ups, silliest dance, most theatrical or loudest. Emcee/host or judges determines the game, and may set time limits.

Judges point to the winning team. Sometimes the audience votes for winner. *(Filler) Tossup*

**Opening Tableau/Closing Tableau.** A line (audience suggestion) that suggests a stage picture. (i.e., lonely in a crowd or embarrassed at a wedding). Then get a second line for the "closing tableau" (e.g. "the car ride home was fun"). *(Narrative) Endowment*

**Opera.** Teams perform an opera about a topic or person suggested from the audience. In an opera, all dialogue is sung. Remember your "Operatic Form" (e.g. *recitative and aria*). See also Gibberish Opera. *(Filler) Music, Culture*

**Opposite Team as Environment.** The opposite team becomes the elements of a suggested environment, remaining onstage while the scene is played. *(Filler) Other Team*

**Opposite Team as Objects.** As your team creates a scene, whenever an object is needed or called for, the opposing team comes in and portrays/ becomes that object. When no longer needed, players leave the stage— ready to become something new. *(Filler) Other Team*

> Give judges status. If they don't have status, what's the point? You really need stern, parental, strict judges.

**Opposite Team Creates Environment.** One at a time the opposite team creates an environment by walking onstage and using or relating to a "space object" that defines an environment, then exits. Your team then comes on and uses the 'environment' created for you. *(Filler) Other Team*

**Order A Coke Scene.** Teams perform a scene, during which they must order a coke. Pretty much anything goes, as long as the coke is ordered during the scene. This can also be played as having to do " *Blank* " during the scene (Kiss, propose, die, reveal a secret, etc.) *(Narrative) Justification, Physical Restriction, Fill in the Blank*

**Ordinary Object.** Also called Prop Transformation. The audience is asked for an ordinary object (real, not space object). Then in the scene, the players use the object in as many different ways as they can, besides its real use. *(Filler) Endowment*

**Orlando Monologue.** The players get an object from the audience and one by one deliver a brief monologue about the object. Often the characters and stories that emerge become intertwined. Three monologues work well. *(Narrative) Narrative, Group*

**Oscar-Winning Moment.** Players get a fictitious title of a movie and begin acting a scene from the movie. The emcee/host calls out one of the player's (or their character's) name and says "Oscar-Winning Moment". That player then begins an Oscar-Winning Moment, the clip that is shown over and over again on entertainment news shows, their 'best" moment in the film, often dramatic or melodramatic in quality. After playing that short clip, the scene resumes. The emcee/host may call out other players or the scene may naturally end. *(Filler) Culture*

> Theatre is the art of stopping people coughing.

**Other Team gets Your Points, Scene Where the.** The title says it all. *(Filer) Other Team*

**Panel Expert Endowment.** Scene in which players are experts. May take the form of a lecture, interview, debate, talk show, family discussion, etc. Players often ask for a topic on which to be an expert. Previous expert introduces the next expert and endows that person with an unusual characteristic and/or expertise. *(Filler) Endowment*

**Party Quirks.** A player goes into the soundproof booth; this player is the host. The audience gives the remaining players quirky character traits (you're obsessed with people's feet, you steal everything you can). The players play a party scene and the host tries to guess what the quirks are. If s/he guesses correctly then that guest must leave and another guest enters. The audience can be encouraged to make encouraging noises (ohhhs and ahhhs) when the host is close to correct. *(Filler) Endowment*

**Pecking Order.** A scene in which (usually) four players play "status". Each player receives a number (from 1 to 4) either by choice, or by chance. Number 1 is highest status and Number 4 is lowest. Orders, messages and other forms of communication and punishment are passed up and down the chain of command. *(Filler) Status*

**Performance Art.** Perform a scene in the style of Performance Art. Lighting technician should feel free to make unusual lighting calls, as nonlinear jumps in thoughts, action, and movement are appropriate. *(Filler) Culture*

**Perspectives.** (Also called **Rashomon**) Team begins a short neutral scene. When the end of that scene is reached, the players repeat the same scene from the perspective of the characters within the scene (three different ways). *(Filler) Psyche*

> **To relate to the audience playfully you have to make mistakes. You have to be imperfect and happy, then the audience will relax.**

**Phone Bank.** Players begin scene as if at a row of pay phones. Player 1 starts an imaginary phone conversation (one-sided) and continues until he/she has established the theme of the conversation. Player 1 then lowers his/her voice and player 2 begins a different phone conversation. When player 2 has established a theme, player 3 begins a new phone conversation. And so on. When all players have established conversations, the players trade focus, using portions of previous conversations (i.e., topics, phrases, names, etc.). After finding the "rhythm" of the conversations, players hang up one by one and end the scene. *(Filler) Group*

**Physical Contact, Speak Only When In.** Players may not speak unless they physically are touching each other. Be strict about that rule, after all, it's the only one. Also called Touch Talk. (K*) *(Filler) Physical Restriction, Technical Zero, Justification*

**Physical Thermometer.** Teammate holds hand in front of player's forehead: Slowly the hand is lowered from head to foot - audience is directed to call "stop" at will. The point where stop is called (the face, rib cage, pelvis, etc.) becomes the 'body lead' of the character. Each player gets a body lead from audience. *(Filler) Justification, Physical Restriction*

**Piano Bar.** Similar to **Panel Expert Endowment** except with songs. Players are 'hanging around' a piano and re- minisce about events in their lives; each singer introduces the next singer and endows that singer with a song subject. *(Filler) Music, Endowment*

**Pillars.** Two pillars are onstage (actually, it does not have to be two pillars, chairs will do just fine). When a player touches a "pillar", the audience supplies the next line of dialogue for that player. **Variation:** Use two audience members as the "pillars" and they supply the line. **Variation:** One "pillar" is for the audience-supplied line, the other pillar, when touched, causes the player to declare an aside to the audience. See also: **Teleprompter.** *(Filler/Narrative)* *Verbal Restriction, Use the Audience*

> **It's got to be playful. It's the relationship between you and the other actors that's important.**

**Pivot.** Imagine the stage is a large disk, balanced on a single point. As a player moves around the stage, his/her weight will affect the balance. Players must compensate for each other on the "pivot", maintaining equilibrium as the scene progresses. (K*) *(Filler) Physical Restriction*

**Platform-Tilt.** Improvisers start a scene simply, without much happening. The players can establish who, what and where...but need to avoid any trouble or anything too interesting. The characters should be 'balanced'. An off-stage voice (emcee/host or other player) calls 'tilt' and the players must change their relationship. Tilt the balance. The off-stage voice can suggest a specific tilt. *(Narrative)* *Endowment, Narrative*

**Play All the Characters in a Scene.** Solo scene. Can ask for a genre. Take time to have reactions to other character(s). Start with one or two characters on stage before you add more. Variation: **Play all the Characters in an Opera.** *(Filler/Narrative) Solo Scene*

**Playbook.** Using an anthology of plays, a player asks for a page number from the audience and turns to that page. The player "holding book" must take all his/her dialogue from that page - in order. Teammates must justify the dialogue in terms of the scene as it plays. *(Filler) Verbal Restriction, Justification*

**Playbook Switch.** Similar to **Playbook** except that whenever the emcee/ host calls "switch" the playbook must change hands on stage and the scene must continue. *(Filler) Verbal Restriction, Justification*

**Poetic Interpretation.** Players pair up; one player speaks naturally and the other player translates in poetic speech. (Similar to **Dubbed Inner Narrative**). *(Filler/Narrative) Verbal Restriction, Culture*

**Poetry.** A scene played to or including Poetry. Maybe a narrative poem. *(Filler) Verbal Restriction*

**Poetry Scene.** A scene played to or including poetry. Maybe a narrative poem. *(Filler) Verbal Restriction, Culture*

**Poetry Speak.** Players play a scene. When the bell sounds (or other appropriate noise maker) the players switch from normal speech to poetic speech. They switch back and forth with every sound of the bell. *(Filler) Verbal Restriction, Culture*

> **Freeze games teach people to get laughs by killing stories.**

**Point of View.** Two people sit in chairs, facing audience. Each does a monologue alternately with the other. They talk about the same situation with different points of view, or talk about their lives and how they have intersected. *(Filler/Narrative) Justification, Narrative, Psyche*

**Point of View Song.** Two or more players get a suggestion of a topic/ issue that there can be many points of view about. Each player sings one verse with his/her point of view. The musician plays the same music for each verse, each player varies their verse by varying their length of phrasing, pitch, pauses, etc. After each player has stepped out to sing their verse, musician plays same music one more time and all players sing at once. *(Filler) Music*

**Police Interrogator.** The person speaking in gibberish is being interrogated by a police officer (speaking English) and the translator translates for the prisoner. (A variation of **Gibberish Interpreter.**) *Verbal Restriction, Justification*

**Pop-Up Book.** One player narrates a story and the other players lie down on the stage (as if pressed in a giant book). The narrator turns a giant page and the players pop up and pose. The narrator pulls tab (or turns a dial, or other typical function of a pop-up book) and the page animates. *(Filler) Physical Restriction, Justification*

**Potpourri.** Each of the players on the team get different verbal (or physical) restrictions (i.e., Player #1: Speak without "I, me, my". Player #2: Speak only in Beatle lyrics. Player #3: Speak only while in physical contact. Player #4: Speak only in one-word sentences.) *(Filler) Endowment, Physical Restriction, Verbal Restriction*

**Present Tense Only, Scene in.** Players create a scene speaking only in Present Tense. You can't reminisce about the past or speculate about the future. *(Filler) Verbal Restriction* Don't swamp the night with musical challenges. Two is okay.

**Prologue.** A player narrates a brief setting for a scene, perhaps giving a basic character introduction. The player lets the scene follow through without narrating it. When the player thinks it's sufficiently over, s/he can close it with an epilogue. *(Narrative) Narrative*

**Prop Transformation.** (Also called **Ordinary Objects, Object from the Audience.**) The audience chooses a prop from among a group that players have brought or the theatre has on hand. Then in the scene, the players use the prop in as many different ways as they can, besides its real use. A hat could become a bowl, and then become a Mask and then become a big ear, a spoon…you get the idea. See if you can keep the story going while the prop transforms. *(Filler) Endowment*

**Questions/Statements Switch.** Scene where players speak with only questions until the emcee/host indicates (by dinging a bell, freezing the players) that they should switch to only statements. The emcee/ host continues to switch the players back and forth from questions to statements. *(Filler) Verbal Restriction, Technical Zero*

**Radio Play.** Players may ask the audience for a genre or decade or anything else inspiring. Voices and sound effects are provided by the players and the movement is as in a radio studio. There may be a sponsor of the show who has jingles; the play could be a continuation of an episodic show where a narrator picks up the story from last week. May be performed in the dark. This scene may need microphones. *(Filler/Narrative) Media, Narrative, Culture*

**Rashomon.** A short scene is played with neutral characters. Then it is replayed from each character's point of view. Hint: It is not necessary to repeat the dialogue exactly. (Based on the movie *Rashomon*) *(Filler/ Narrative) Psyche*

**Realistic Scene.** Players attempt to play a scene as realistically as possible. *(Narrative) Narrative*

**Reality Freeze.** (Also called **Location Freeze**). Play a scene. The emcee/host calls out "freeze" and asks the audience for a location. A new scene begins in the new location using new characters, justifying the body suggestions from the freeze. *(Filler) Endowment, Justification, Jump*

**Reminiscence Scene.** One or more players reminisce about an event or person in the past. Teammates may act out the memories in a split-focus scene. *(Filler/Narrative) Jump, Psyche*

**Replay.** (Also called **Genre Replay**). After a short neutral scene, the next two "replays" of that scene are in a genre, in the style of a playwright or a film director. The last replay can be a musical style. See **Styles**. *(Filler) Justification*

**Reverse, Scene in.** A scene starts at the end and continues to the beginning. Actions, conversations and all cause and effect relationships are reversed. Sentences are still spoken forwards. Also known as Backwards Scene. (K*) *(Filler) Physical Restriction*

> **When using the audience, bring them to the stage, take them back, treat them well. This generates good will. The thing you need most is a benevolent audience. Treat them right. Create benevolence. Use an audience member at least once per half.**

**Rewrite History.** Replay a famous moment in history. Because it's improvised, it will turn out differently. *(Filler) Culture*

**Ritual Scene.** Players create a scene enacting a ritualistic activity based on an everyday object or activity. *(Filler) Physical Restriction, Culture*

**Sandwiches, Drinks, Cars & Materials.** Each player gets a type of one of the above and bases their character on the characteristics of that specific sandwich, drink, car or material. For example a character based on "burlap" meets a character based on "French dip". Players could ask for anything for which there are many (a clothing designer, baseball team, subject in high school, anything) *(Filler) Endowment*

**Scene, Song, Scene.** A musical scene that starts with dialogue then breaks into song and then goes back into dialogues before it ends. The idea is that the challenge is similar to a Broadway musical where the song emerges from the action and emotion. *(Narrative) Music*

**Suggestions are only to make the audience partially responsible. Don't always ask for them.**

**Scene that Starts Immediately after Getting a Suggestion.** After a team gets their suggestion, the lights don't go down and the players don't dash off to the side: they start the scene right then and there... from where they are. *(Filler/Narrative)*

**Secret Endowment.** Two players in turn face upstage and plug their ears. Player A asks audience for a secret about Player B; B does the same for Player A (i.e., he wears a toupee; she writes for the National Enquirer). In the scene, the players endow each other with their secret. Usually a three-minute timed scene. *(Filler) Endowment, Timed*

**Secret Word Endowment.** Team members face upstage and plug their ears. emcee/host asks the audience for a word for each of them. Using sheets of paper, a big marking pen, and tape, emcee/host places a word on each of the players' backs. Players play a scene and try to get teammates to say the "secret word" on his/her own back. Usually a three-minute timed scene. *(Filler) Endowment, Timed*

**Seductions.** A scene in which someone is seduced. *(Narrative) Justification*

**Sentence Scenes.** Players may only use a specified number of words for each sentence they speak, usually between one and seven. Each player may have his or her own limit. See these number scenes: **Step-Word Scene, Countdown, Three Word Sentences.** *(Filler) Verbal Restriction, Technical Zero*

**Serious Scene.** Play a scene as seriously as possible. When the audience laughs (giggles don't count), the scene is over. See **Laugh 'N Go, Delay the Laugh**. *(Narrative) Narrative*

**Sex Role Reversal.** The men are played by women (as men) and the women are played by men (as women). Also called **Gender Reversal**. *(Filler) Justification*

**Shakespearean Scene.** The players create a scene that uses Shakespearean language (verse and grammatical forms), characters, plots and conventions. Can also get a modern-day situation but use Shakespearean forms. *(Filler/ Narrative) Culture, Verbal Restriction*

> Expect the unexpected so you can change in front of the eyes of the audience; it will look real and truthful.

**Shrinking-and-Growing Machine.** The reverse of a **Growing and Shrinking Machine**. Starting with a four-player scene and "shrinking" to a one-player scene then "growing" to a four-player scene. The scene can start with frozen positions (i.e., stopped dance or statues). (See **Growing-and-Shrinking Machine.**) *(Filler) Jump, Justification*

**Side-Coach Challenge**. Scene where one (or more) of the players is selected to side coach the scene (the side-coach makes suggestions throughout the scene as to what the players do). *(Filler/Narrative)*

**Sideways Scene**. Scene in which the actual floor of the stage is used as a wall and an imaginary floor is established parallel to the downstage edge of the stage. (K*) *(Filler) Physical Restriction*

**Silent Movie.** Scene in the style of a silent movie. Your musician and a lighting improviser add to the style. *(Filler) Scene Without Words, Culture, Verbal Restriction*

**Silent Scene.** (Similar to **Scene Without Words.**) Scene without dialogue, music, sound effects or any utterance. *(Narrative) Scene Without Words, Verbal Restriction*

**Sing About It!** A scene in which anyone from the audience can shout out "Sing About It!" during the scene and the players then sing about whatever they were just talking about. This can happen multiple times during the scene. *(Filler) Music*

**Slide Show.** A player or players show 'slides' from an event, and the slides are created by other players forming a tableau. Players have the option of announcing what is on the slide before they call for 'next slide' or justifying the positions in the tableau. You can also invite audience members to participate. *(Filler) Physical Restriction, Justification, Group*

> **Get the Emcee off the stage. The stage belongs to the actors.**

**Slips Of Paper.** Slips of paper with lines of dialogue are spread randomly on the floor (or shuffled and divided up among the players). At any time during the scene, players read a slip of paper aloud as their next line of dialogue. The lines of dialogue can be from anywhere. Sources can be: the audience (gather them before the show), random quotes from Shakespeare or lines from Beatle songs, etc. This one takes preparation time. The slips of paper could also have genres, character qualities, tilts, status behaviors or office jargon. See **Stage Directions**. *(Filler) Media, Justification*

**Slow Motion Commentary.** Players act out an activity, event (an everyday event) or encounter in extreme slow motion, while other players supply sports-style commentary at normal speed (one can provide "color", that is background information, stats, etc.; the other can provide "action" commentary). See also **Status Exchange Commentary** and **Narrative Scene Commentary**. *(Filler) Physical Restriction, Justification*

**Small Voice.** (Also called **Scene with the Little Voice** and **Speck**) A player enters scene, a small voice speaks (offstage player's voice) and the player relates to the source of the little voice. The player immediately endows the small voice and relates to it. ("Oh, a tiny talking acorn!") Often the small voice has a problem and the player helps to solve it. (Good for wafflers and wimpers.) (K*) *(Narrative) Narrative, Other* **Bodies**

**Solo Scene.** Scene in which only one player is onstage. Teammates may supply him/her with voices, props and sound effects. You can sing a song, make a speech or give a preacher's sermon. Many, many, many games can be adapted for Solo Scenes. See **SoundScape, Play All the Characters in the Scene, Truth to Lie, "No, You Didn't!"** *(Narrative) Physical Restriction, Solo Scene*

**Something, Scene From.** The players improvise a scene based only on an audience suggestion (or object or something). *(Narrative) Fill in the Blank*

**Song.** Players improvise a song about a topic supplied by the audience. blues, doo-wop, torch song, gospel, folk, hoe-down anything is possible. Try out solos, duets, or group songs (can use a "chorus, stanza, chorus" format for a group). Go on, be daring! *(Filler) Music*

**Song Cue.** Musical scene in which the song titles are the line of dialogue just said. Emcee/Host or musician indicates which line by ringing a bell, blowing whistle, or calling out "song cue". A short song is sung and the scene continues. *(Filler/Narrative) Music*

**Song Lyrics.** One or more players may only speak in song lyrics. Note: Use already existing songs, not 'made-up' songs. Variation: **Lines from Movies:** One or more players can only speak in lines from movies. *(Filler) Verbal Restriction,*

**Sound Effects Scene.** A tape with randomly placed sound effects (every 30 or so seconds) is played while a scene is being played. Players must incorporate and justify the sound effects in terms of the scene as it plays. If you have a sound improviser, they can provide live sound effects. A related game is **Foley Room**. *(Filler) Justification*

**Sounds Like a Song**. The players play a scene and anytime a player says 'sing about it' to another player, that player must sing about what they were just talking about. This can

happen multiple times. (Similar to **Sing About It!**) *(Filler)*
*Music*

## Do one-on-one scenes. It is a change.

**SoundScape.** One or more players act out a scene, with vocal sound effects provided by offstage players. (K*) *(Filler/Narrative) Justification*

**Space Jump.** Similar to **Growing-and-Shrinking Machine**, but the emcee/host chooses the order in which the scenes are repeated, by shouting out the corresponding number. (Offstage players have their backs to scene). *(Filler/Narrative) Jump*

**Speaking in One Voice.** Players get into groups of two (or more) and speak in one voice as one character. So two players could be the employer and the other two players could be the employee. See also **Story in One Voice.** *(Filler) Group, Verbal Restriction*

**Speaking in Turn, Scene.** Players decide an order and then must speak in that order during the scene. Take your time. *(Filler) Verbal Restriction, Technical Zero*

## People love watching mime, actors hate doing it.

**Spelling Bee.** A gibberish word is solicited from the audience. It is then spelled and defined by a player. Then a short scene is played demonstrating the word's definition. Each player on the team may spell a word. *(Filler) Justification*

**Spelling scene.** All words must be spelled during the course of the s-c- e-n-e. *(Filler) Verbal Restriction*

**Spendthrift**. Each player gets a number from the audience. During the scene, that number is the total number of words that the player may use. *(Filler) Verbal Restriction*

**Split-Focus Scene.** A scene in which the focus alternates back and forth between characters and scenes in different areas of the stage. The scenes may or may not be related, but some elements of one scene should be incorporated in the other. *(Filler/Narrative) Group*

**Split Screen.** Imagine the stage split down the middle. Play the scene as if Stage Right were Stage Left and conversely Stage Left were Stage Right. Two-person scene is played and different players perform stage right and stage left. *(Filler) Physical Restriction*

**Stage Directions.** Stage directions taken from plays are put on multiple slips of paper and then randomly distributed around the stage. The players play a scene and occasionally reach down, pick up a stage direction and follow the instruction on the slip of paper. Similar to **Slips of Paper**. Hint: prepare the slips of paper ahead of time. *(Filler)*

**Standing, Sitting, Kneeling, Lying Down**. During the scene, players may stand, sit, kneel or lie down; however, no two players may be in anyone of these positions at the same time. Audience should be cued to "Ooh" and "Aah" if two players are in the same position at the same time.

Variation: **Sitting, Kneeling, Standing, Off Stage**. (Filler) Physical Restriction, Technical Zero, Justification

**Starting With Interpretive Dance, Scene**. Scene starts with a short musical interlude. One or more players dance to the music. After 30 seconds or so, emcee/host blows the whistle or the music stops, the dancers freeze, and then begin a scene justifying their current body positions. See: **Music, Scene From**. *(Filler) Music, Justification*

**State Trooper**. (Alt. Name: **Highway Patrol**.) A state trooper interrogates a driver about why s/he was speeding while the passenger is in a sound- proof booth. The driver tells his/her elaborate story. The trooper then interrogates the passenger. The driver mimes the story to the passenger who attempts to re-tell the story without letting the trooper know that he/she is getting clues from behind the troopers back. Three minute timed scene (the first minute is the explanation and the last two are the passenger trying to guess). *(Filler) Endowment, Timed*

> **Judge yourself by checking in with your partner. If your partner is having a good time with you, then you're on the right track. If you're good but no one likes you, go solo. If you're not so good but people want to play with you, you'll get better.**

**Statues**. Audience members mold players' bodies into positions (statues). The players begin the scene, justifying those positions. Players may be required to end the scene in the same positions. *(Filler) Other Bodies, Justification*

**Status Exchange Commentary**. Similar to **Slow Motion Commentary** but with a focus on status. Commentator, "He's toughing his face and avoiding eye contact, he's losing status." Hint: It could involve a lot of give-and-take between the actors and the commentators instead of one always leading the other. *(Filler/Narrative) Status, Justification*

**Status Slide**. As each player speaks, his/her character status goes a little lower until the lowest possible status is obtained, then the next speaker goes to the top (highest status). The slide-cycle is begun again. *(Filler) Status*

**Status Switch**. A timed, pecking order scene. The characters have a definite hierarchy to their status, the highest status character is number 1 and subsequently lower status characters have higher numbers. During the scene the character with the highest status (1) becomes the character with the lowest status (4) – and vice versa. Character with status number 3 becomes a number 2 and number 2 becomes a number 3. Naturally, the change in status must be justified. This can be played where the emcee/ host calls for the change at some point in the scene. *(Filler) Status, Justification, Timed*

**Games come from theory. Want new games? Get a new theory. If it doesn't work, scrap it.**

**Status Tower.** A player comes onstage starting either at high status or low status, and as each player enters they take a status higher or lower than the previous player, depending upon which way the status tower is headed. (K*) *(Filler) Status*

**Status Transfer**. Two players start out with different status, and gradually change (transfer) to the other player's condition. A time limit may be in order for this scene. (K*) *(Filler) Status, Justification, Timed*

**Status Zones**. The stage is divided into a high status side and a low status side. (A variation of Zones.) *(Filler) Physical Restriction, Status, Justification*

**Step-Word Scene**. Scene begins with a one-word sentence. The next sentence is a two-word sentence, then a three-word sentence, a four-word sentence, and so on, until the scene reaches ten-word sentences. Then the players must use nine-word sentences, eight, seven, all the way back down to a one-word sentence-- which ends the scene. See **Countdown**. *(Filler) Verbal Restriction, Technical Zero*

**Stimulus/Response**. Plugging ears and humming, team members are secluded as, one at a time, each member gets a response s/he will have to another teammate's behavior. "If Carl touches his face, I'll say something reassuring." "Whenever Dan smiles, I will faint." "If Sarah uses the word 'I', I'll ask her if 'she's alright'." "Whenever Patty mentions love, I'll get nervous and speak in a Canadian accent." Each player has a response to another player so that everyone is watching someone else. *(Filler) Justification, Physical Restriction*

**Stop & Go**. Freeze while talking and move while silent or vice versa. *(Filler) Physical Restriction, Technical Zero*

**Stop-Action Narrative**. Scene begins with a narrator starting a scene and the other players moving the action ahead. At points during the scene, the narrator may stop the scene and ask the audience where the story goes next, either with a "who walks in the door?" question, or a question that leads the narrative more, such as: "Mary does not know that John has a secret. What is that secret?" The narrator is not usually a character in the story. (K*) *(Filler) Fill in the Blank*

**Story from the Audience**. See '**Day in the Life**'. Ask the audience for a story and then play the story onstage. (K*) *(Filler/Narrative) Fill in the Blank, Narrative, Use the Audience*

**Story In One Voice**. The team stands center stage and tells a story in one voice (speaking simultaneously) based on an audience suggestion. See also the scene: **Speaking In One Voice**. *(Filler) Verbal Restriction, Group*

> **All games should be played wrong. If you can play it wrong, you can play it right.**

**Story-Story-Die**. Players stand in a line onstage. Emcee/Host points to one player who begins to tell a story. Emcee/Host points to a different player who must take up the story at exactly the point in the story where it left off. Players may not repeat the last word, pause, stutter, or in any way "boff" the story. If s/he does, the audience shouts "DIE" and that player is eliminated. (Before the game begins, let the audience practice yelling, "DIE!") Play continues until only one player is left, who may finish the story. This is the ultimate toss-up game. Optional death scenes may be granted. Can be played without the "die" rule in effect as a narrative challenge. See also **Different Story-Story-Die, One-Word Story Sung Story-Die**, and **Story-Story-Die with Different Styles**. *(Filler) Narrative, Tossup, Group*

**Story-Story-Die with Different Styles**. Each player gets a story style from the audience. The players play Story-Story-Die with each player changing the story style without changing the story. *(Filler) Toss-up, Group*

**Storybook**. Similar to **Pop-up Book** except without the animation. One player narrates a story and the other players pose as if they're the illustrations in the book. Think of it as a combination of **Narrated Story** and **Slide Show**. *(Narrative) Physical Restriction, Justification, Group, Narrative*

**Straight Man**. Scene where one player is designated as the "straight man". In this case "straight man" refers to the role of a member of a comedy team, where one person delivers the set-up lines and the other gets all the laughs. *(Filler) Culture*

> The ones who have done it for years are under
> the most stress because they're supposed to
> do well.

**String of Pearls**. (Also known as **Book Ends.**) This game seems to work best with a lot of people. Players get two unconnected "lines". One player step forward and gives the first line of a story, a second player steps forward and provides the unconnected last line of a story. They then restate their lines from "beginning to end". As each other player steps forward and adds a line, the entire story gets "reread". Players can put their line anywhere in the sequence. By the end all the necessary lines will have been added so that the story makes sense. **Variation**: players can add more than one line to the story. *(Filler/Narrative) Group*

**Strong Emotions, Scene With**. Each player gets a strong emotion from the audience and plays that emotion strongly. *(Filler/Narrative) Justification*

**Stunt Double**. Players begin a scene. At any point during the scene, onstage player may call out "Stunt Double!" and be replaced by a stunt person for any dangerous or distasteful activities. Stunt Doubles call out "First Team" to be replaced by players, who continue the story. Can also be done as **Stunt Double Musical**. *(Filler) Physical Restriction*

**Styles (3-Scene)**. Players perform a short neutral scene. When the end of that scene is reached, the players repeat the same scene in three different ways. Players ask for a period in history, a playwright, and an artist. (Play the scene as if: in the future, written by Shakespeare, painted by Norman Rockwell.) **Variation: 3 SCENE**: Players ask for 3 emotions, and play the scene stressing those emotions.

See also **Perspectives (Rashomon), Replay** and **Musical Rashomon**. *(Filler) Justification*

**Sub-Personalities**. A two-person scene. Player A has two sub- personalities, given by the audience and played by other actors. During the scene, these "sub-personalities" may take the place of Player A and continue the scene until Player A thinks s/he should re-enter. When Player A replaces the "sub-personality", s/he must justify the mood swing. *(Filler) Psych*

> **The more you think, the less you perceive.**

**Subtitles**. Scene starts in gibberish. Offstage player runs across the stage and "translates" for the scene. This can be **Opera Subtitles** for a **Gibberish Opera**. *(Filler) Verbal Restriction*

**Sung Story-Die** (Alt Name: **Song Song Die**) Players stand in a line onstage. Emcee/Host points to one player who begins to improvise a song. Emcee/Host points to a different player who must continue singing the song. If a player stumbles the audience shouts "die" and that player is eliminated. Play continues until only one player is left, who may finish the song. This can be played without a musician. See **Story-Story-Die**. *(Filler) Narrative, Tossup, Music*

**Supply the Word**. Two audience volunteers are solicited and assigned a teammate as a partner. The audience members are instructed to supply the word whenever their partner hesitates or searches for a word. See also **Pillars. Variation: Teleprompter:** the audience member silently "mouths" a line to the player. *(Filler) Fill in the Blank, Use the Audience, Justification*

**Survival.** You throw an improviser on the stage and say, "the lights will go out in two minutes", leave them there and watch them survive. *(Filler) Timed*

**Tableau from History.** This Tossup is to see which team can recreate a moment from history (e.g. Washington crossing the Delaware) in a short time frame (e.g. 20 seconds). Audience gets to applaud for the winning group that best captures the moment. *(Filler) Tossup, Timed, Culture*

**Tableau to Scene.** From a tableau of players, three come out and speak of who they are, what they want. After the third the scene starts up. Can be the start to a Shakespearean scene. See also **Yearbook Photo Montage**. *(Filler) Endowment, Justification*

**Tag Team Monologue.** A player starts a monologue and other players on his/her team tag in, take the same physical positions, accent, and gesture and, continue the monologue while keeping in "character" as set up by first player. If you get a suggestion, ask for a topic or the name of this character. *(Narrative) Group*

> The theatre is full of people who want to be on the stage but don't want to be in the scene.

**Technical Zero-Advanced Score.** (Also called the **Kreskin Challenge**) A player takes a blank piece of paper (show audience) and writes a number (between 0 and 15) but does not show the audience or fellow teammates. The paper is sealed in an envelope and placed in view of the audience. A scene is played and scored by the judges. If the combined score matches the pre-written number, the team gets the points; if not, the team gets "0". *(Filler) Technical Zero*

**Teleprompter.** Two audience volunteers are solicited and join the players on stage. The audience members are instructed to silently "mouth" a line to the player, whenever a player looks to them as if searching for a word. The players say the line they 'think' the audience member said. See also **Supply the Word** and **Pillars**. *(Filler) Fill in the Blank, Use the Audience, Justification*

**Thirty Seconds of Silence, Start with.** The scene must start with 30 seconds of silence. The emcee/host can announce when the 30 seconds is up. Hint: have the reason for not talking be about the relationship. *(Filler/ Narrative) Verbal Restriction, Justification*

**Three-Act Play.** Players get a suggestion for a title of a play that has never been done before. Then they get one audience member to put the numbers 1, 2, and 3 into any order they like (2-1-3 or 3-1-2 or even 1-2-3). Then the play is done with the acts in this order. *(Filler/Narrative) Narrative*

**Three-Way Dubbing.** Players A, B & C start a scene. A speaks for B, B speaks for C and C speaks for A. You can also try **Four-Way Dubbing**. Also known as **Cross-Talk**. (For just two players, see **Doublespeak**. *(Filler) Verbal Restriction*

**Three-Word Sentences.** Players can only speak in three-word sentences. See also X-word Sentences. *(Filler) Verbal Restriction, Filler*

**Through the Ages**. Similar to a **Styles** scene. Ask for three periods in history. Players then ask for just about anything-for instance: a family. Then we see that family as they might exist in each of those periods (the dynamics, the concerns, the status, etc.) *(Filler/Narrative) Jump, Justification*

**Time Machine**. A scene involving time jumps and reality jumps. A player or the emcee/host may call out "flashback" at any time. The players must then move the scene in time or reality as in "that reminds me of the time when..." When the flashback is over, a player or the emcee/host may call out "reality check", and the scene reverts to its pre-flashback moment. *(Filler) Jump*

**Time to Do Scene**. Scene takes as long as the length of time of an activity (i.e., Scene In the Time It Takes A Match To Burn Out, or Scene As Long As My Teammate's Head is In A Bucket of Water, or Scene In The Length Of Time It Takes To Go Next Door and Get a Cheeseburger, that sort of thing). *(Filler) Timed*

> **People pay money to see people on stage altered and alter each other.**

**Timed Scene**. Broad definition of any scene that has a specified time limit. Timed Scenes are not limited to measurements of the clock (1 Minute Scene, 90 Second Scene, etc.); the time limit can be the length of time of an activity (see **Time to Do Scene**.) Can just perform a scene or try other timed scenes: **Blank in a Minute, Death in a Minute, Love in a Minute, Epic in a Minute, Half Life, Movie in a Minute, Fairy Tale in a Minute, Most Justified Exits and Entrances in a Minute, Opera in Three Minutes,** This show in a Minute, all sorts of possibilities. (K*) *(Filler) Timed*

**Timed Styles**. Players improvise a 6 line scene, then repeat it as many times as possible in different styles within a 3 minute time period. After each style players ask the audience for a new style. Does the dialogue have to be the same each

time? Depends on how you want to play the game. *(Filler)*
*Timed*

**Tossup Games.** At times during Theatresports™ matches,
it is necessary to have a "winner" quickly and decisively
determined. Reasons for this are varied: to determine who
plays first, to break a tie, or just a way to vary the entertainment for the evening. There are many games
that can be used as a Toss-up. Also, playing "Rock/ Paper/
Scissors" (a.k.a. Rochambeau), holding your breath for the
longest time and flipping a coin are valid (and useful)
possibilities. *(Filler) Toss-Up*

**Touch Talk.** Players may not speak unless they physically
are touching each other. Be strict about that rule, after all, it's
the only one. Variation: Each touch has to be to a different
part of the body. And it has to be meaningful. Also called
**Speak Only when in Physical Contact**. *(Filler) Physical
Restriction, Technical Zero, Justification*

> **Focusing on your partner distracts you and it
> might help free you up.**

**True Feelings.** Players or a player must speak with his/her
true feelings. This could be triggered by a bell, the music, or
the Host. *(Filler) Psyche*

**Truth to Lie.** (Solo Scene) A player starts out with a true
story from his/her own life. The goal is to seamlessly add in
a significant "lie" that totally changes the story. It should all
seem so truthful that the audience cannot tell where the lie
occurred in the story. *(Filler) Solo Scene*

**TV Channel.** A player gets several different types of television stations from the audience and then randomly shouts

these out during the scene. The other players must immediately change the style of the scene without changing the story. OR this can be played as a freeze scene, where the players must justify their "frozen" positions in the new channel's genre. (PBS, ESPN, FOX, MTV, Religious, Shopping Channel, Public Access, Kid's Channel, etc.) *(Filler) Media Challenge, Justification*

**TV Guide**. Have an audience member draw from the pre-cut descriptions of movies (with the title of the movie cut or crossed out), read the description and then create a scene based upon that description. **Variation:** Set the scene in different genres or musical styles. See **Media Challenge** and **Newspaper Headline**. *(Narrative) Justification, Narrative*

**Two Chairs.** Player places two chairs on the stage and asks the audience, "Where are these two chairs?" The scene begins. Not to be confused with **Chair**: a Tossup game. *(Filler) Fill in the Blank*

**Two-Headed Mutant.** See also **One-Word-at-a-Time Scene**. Two players tell a story one word-at-a-time and act it out as they go along. *(Narrative) Verbal Restriction*

**TXT ME.** A player gives out his/her mobile phone number and encourages audience members to text them lines of dialogue during an improvised scene. Player or players carry their mobile phone and improvise a scene using and justifying the suggested lines. Variation: Borrow a phone from an audience member and use one of their txt conversations as the lines in a scene. *(Filler) Verbal REstriction, Justification*

**Typewriter.** Narrative game, in which one player sits at an imaginary desk and "types" (narrates) a story while members of his/her team act out the story. You can play with using "white out" or "deleting" or rewriting a passage. (K*) *(Narrative)* Narrative

**Understudy.** (A variation of **Actor Switch**) One player stands upstage in a "soundproof booth" while a scene takes place. At some point the "lead" in the scene takes ill and departs, the "understudy" is tagged in and the rest of the cast endows that player with the entire story. *(Filler/ Narrative)* *Endowment*

**Using a Member of the Audience, Scene.** Ask for a volunteer from the audience and then use him/her in a scene with the other players. Let them improvise! Remember to get their name, introduce them to the teammates and to the audience... and treat them well. (K*) *(Filler)* *Use the Audience*

> **The obvious is wonderful. The audience is so pleased when you're obvious; you'll be 'one of them'.**

**Using Character or Plot Line from Previous Scene.** The title says it all. *(Filler/Narrative)* *Narrative*

**Verse, Scene in.** Scene in which players use verse as they speak. Unless specified, the verse does not need to be rhymed couplets. Other poetic forms are allowable (i.e., Iambic Pentameter, Haiku, Free Verse, Limerick, etc.) (K*) *(Filler)* *Verbal Restriction, Culture*

**Voice-over.** When each player enters the scene they freeze and the opposite team gives a quick voice-over about the character or relationship. *(Filler)* *Endowment, Justification*

**What Am I Wearing?** The players ask the audience for suggestions of how they are dressed and then play a scene as if they are so dressed. *(Filler/Narrative)* *Endowment, Justification*

**What Are You Doing?** Player A starts an action- for instance: Sautéing Vegetables. Player B says: "What are you doing?" Player A responds with an activity *different* from what he/she is doing: " I'm knitting". Player B begins to mime knitting. Player A then asks: "What are you doing?". Player B then would respond with something different, such as: "Dancing on the head of a pin." This pattern continue until one player hesitates, cannot respond, responds with the action that they have done or are doing (or something very close). *(Filler)* *Tossup*

**What Are You Doing Tomorrow?** Solicit from the audience someone's plans for tomorrow, and then play the scene. Could be done in a theatre style or nightmare or... See **Day in the Life**. *(Filler/Narrative)* *Use the Audience, Narrative*

**What If "Blank"?** Audience fills in the blank: "What if '*Blank?*'", with something like "What if money did actually grow on trees?" *(Filler/ Narrative)* *Fill in the Blank*

> You can think of improv as an exercise in being good-natured.

**With (A) "*Blank*", Scene.** Another Fill in the Blank scene. May be filled in by the audience, or filled in by the emcee/host, or challenging team. The answer to any question could provide the 'blank'. *(Filler/Narrative)* *Fill in the Blank*

**With One Character on Stage At A Time, Scene.** The

name says it all. You could also try with "Blank" number of Players on Stage At All Times. *(Narrative) Physical Restriction*

**With Only Questions, Scene.** Do you understand this scene? Can you tell that no one is allowed to make a statement? Is there any way to make this game clearer? *(Filler) Verbal Restriction, Technical Zero*

**Without (a) "*Blank*", Scene.** May be filled in by the audience, or filled in by the emcee/host challenging team. *(Filler/Narrative) Fill in the Blank*

**Without Contractions, Scene**. The players perform a scene without contractions. If ~~you're~~ you are cool, ~~don't~~ do not let us stop ~~you'all~~ you! (Hint: Try to speak normally.) *(Filler) Verbal Restriction*

**Without Questions, Scene.** Play this game without asking any questions. Can also be played as a timed challenge where the emcee/host calls out "Switch" and the players change from a Scene Without Questions to a Scene With Only Questions. See also *Questions/Statements Switch*. *(Filler) Verbal Restriction, Technical Zero, Timed*

> **It's all about taking the audience along on the journey. Keep it simple. Take one idea and develop it.**

**Without the Letter "*Blank*", Scene.** Players ask for a letter, and no one is allowed to use a word containing that letter. The more common the letter (e.g. "S"), the more fun that will ensue. (K\*) *(Filler) Fill in the Blank, Verbal Restriction*

**Without the Word "I", Scene.** Verbal restriction scene. No player may say the word "I" or "eye" or "aye". *(Filler) Verbal Restriction, Technical Zero*

**Word-at-a-Time Expert.** Two or more players stand side-by-side and answer questions on a given subject of expertise, one word-at-a-time. Another player may act as a presenter (often in the style of TV talk show) and solicit questions from the audience for the expert. *(Filler) Verbal Restriction*

**Word-at-a-Time Expert with Audience Member.** A variation of **Word- at-a-Time Expert** with an audience member as one of the players in the "line up" supplying words for the expert. *(Filler) Use the Audience, Verbal Restriction*

**Word-at-a-Time Narrator.** Two or more players stand side by side and narrate the story one word-at-a-time while the other players act it out. *(Filler/Narrative) Narrative, Verbal Restriction*

**Word-at-a-Time Story.** Players stand in a line downstage and tell a word-at-a-time story (each speak one word in sequence). Based on an audience suggestion. *(Narrative) Group, Verbal Restriction*

**Words, Sounds and Silence (or Speak, Grunt and Shut up).** In one zone players can speak. In the second zone players can only make noises. In the third zone players must be silent. (See **Zones**.) *(Filler) Verbal Restriction, Physical Restriction, Justification*

**World Would be a Better Place if "*Blank*", The.** Ask the audience to fill the "blank" then play the scene as if it were so! *(Filler/Narrative) Fill in the Blank*

**X-Word Scene.** Scene has the same number of words per sentence until the emcee/host calls a new number; the scene continues with that number of words per sentence until the emcee/host calls a new number. The emcee/host may go to the audience for some or all of the numbers. (Also known as

**"N" Word Sentences**. See also **Three Word Sentences**.) (K*) *(Filler) Verbal Restriction*

**Yearbook Photo Montage.** Get a suggestion from the audience for a yearbook picture grouping (e.g. the "Drama Club", "The Young Republicans", etc.). On a signal, all players freeze into the photo position. One by one, each steps out and speaks a very brief monologue, telling their name and something about why they are in the club. You can also "fast forward" from freshman year to senior year with the same participants. *(Filler/Narrative) Endowment, Justification*

> **In life we are obedient and safe. On stage we are naughty, risky and dangerous.**

**Yearbook Photo Montage to Scene.** The montage (above) can also go into a narrative game in which a story is developed using characters created in the monologues. *(Filler/Narrative) Endowment, Justification*

**"Yes . . . Sounds good to me . . . I'll go along with that."** Play a scene where one person's lines are written on a piece of paper. They are "Yes. Sounds good to me. I'll go along with that. Great", often played with a member of the audience. (K*) *(Filler/Narrative) Use the Audience, Verbal Restriction*

**Variation: No, Fuck off, Shut up, Leave me alone, and Forget it.** Play a scene where one person's lines are written on a piece of paper. They are as noted in the title of this game, often played with a member of the audience. *(Filler/Narrative) Use the Audience, Verbal Restriction*

**Yesterday.** Every time the word "yesterday" is said, the

scene changes to the day before and that scene is played. (Hint: This works best when the number of scenes to be played is set beforehand.) *(Filler/Narrative) Jump*

> **Some games aren't worth playing without risk because they depend on failure.**

**You Can't Complete Any...** Scene where you can't complete any sentences. Someone can finish it for you, or it can trail off, or you can interrupt yourself or someone else. *(Filler) Verbal Restriction*

**Zones.** Players divide stage into sections (zones) and get suggestions for each zone. Players play the scene and as they move from zone to zone, they take on the qualities of that zone. Zone suggestions: Emotional Zones, Genre Zones, Historical Periods, Alliteration, Body Parts, **Status Zones**. (Also known as **Quadrants**.) See **Words, Sounds and Silence**. *(Filler) Fill in the Blank, Physical Restriction, Justification*

> **The pressure and the fear will make you more verbal and keep you away from emotion.**
>
> **You must learn to:**
>
> • **yield control**
>
> • **take control when you have to**
>
> • **work for the other person**
>
> • **avoid working harder**
>
> `**In the end the thing of most value to us is you bringing yourself (your world, fears, dreams, association, etc.) to the stage.**

# Keith Johnstone
# Notes on the games.

Keith Johnstone and Rebecca Stockley had several conversations about the games in an earlier edition of the Playbook. Some of his comments have been incorporated into the current playbook and some we felt should be passed on to you just as Keith said them.

**Actor Switch.** That should come under substitutions. If the actor suddenly feels unhappy, they should just make the time-out sign and be substituted. The description is long winded and complicated. It's not really a game.

**After Hours.** Oh, I hate After Hours.

**Alliteration.** Detestable. Basically stupid.

**Alliteration Die.** Categories is much better than Alliteration Die.

**Alphabet.** I don't like it. Play it once - don't play it for a year. Never lock yourself into doing the whole alphabet.

**Animal People.** Animal families is quite interesting. Have a family all one animal. If it won't develop have one of the characters lose it and go completely animal.

**Arms.** Don't add other games to it. (Experts.) Don't play it too often... once a month. Arms are very good talking to the audience as one person. Two people relating to each other as people is lovely. Cut the scene before the audience dies out.

**Asides.** Not really a game - more of a procedure. Don't keep the soft freeze - it is too formal and inhibiting.

**Attitude.** Never display the attitude to the audience.

**Audience, Scene Using.** Never use an audience member if you can't make them look really good. If you don't make them look good, apologize to them. Always invite them on the stage if you don't want them (because ---it's going so well).

**Ballet.** Don't call it ballet - call it dance. Only do it when truly elated - don't do it when faking enthusiasm. Works best as modern dance with highbrow commentary. Good to give pretentious title like The Coming of Spring.

**Bedtime Story.** Doesn't look like a game to me. It's just a scene. It would be much more fun to have the kid go to sleep and dream a story.

**Best "Blank" Scene.** Cut best "blank" out - it's crap.

**Blank in a Minute.** I detest the ideas of an actor making an omelet in a minute, but I love the idea of throwing an improviser on the stage for a minute and not tell him what to do.

**Boris.** It is an advanced game. Be willing to cut it short. See description in Improv for Storytellers. The prisoner is a cringing coward desperate to talk. The interrogator shouldn't control the reaction of the prisoner - say "Help him, Boris" rather than "twist his leg, Boris".

**Chain Murder.** Yuck. It is a terrible lock-in.

**Chair.** Yawn.

**Chance of a Lifetime.** Smiling Face.

**Character Traits from the Audience.** Okay as a whim.

Don't do it too often. Reject any character traits they don't want to do.

**Clashing Environments.** Traditional game. The example given is appalling. Better example. You're in your living room, and you're on stage with a person at a bus-stop. You want something ordinary.

**Close Up/ Long Shot.** Yuck.

*Commercial. Beginners should avoid.* Yuck.

**Connect the Lines**. Yuck. Encourages bridging. I don't understand why you would play that.

**Consciences.** Smiley face.

**Continuation.** Just let the other team tap when they're ready rather than timing the scene or freezing it.

**Cutting Room.** Smiley when it goes forward in time. Yuck when it is used for side tracking.

**Day in the Life.** Smiley when they tell what they did that day.

**Death in a Minute.** Smiley. Add "start loving each other" or "start as non- murderers". Add that the death should be at the beginning.

**Delay the Laugh.** You're competing to see who can stay on for the longest time. A spin off from the Gerbil Game (See Keith Johnstone Newsletter).

**Doublespeak.** Smiley. Keep it short. Play at the end of dubbing scenes.

**Dub our Musical** or **Musical Dub.** Excellent if used to move the scene forwards. One of Loose Moose's most successful scenes with audience members as people on stage.

**Dubbing.** Keep very short. **Smiley. Repeat with two emotional body parts. Under 30 seconds.**

**Ending in "Blank". Yuck.**

**Emotional Transfer.** Keith calls this a Transformation Game; you can also transfer speed. The status transfer is Keith's; the emotional transfer is from Spolin's.

**Film Rollback.** Good to do as a procedure but it isn't a game.

**Fingers.** Good for science fiction. Tedious if it goes on too long. Fingers should be maniacally happy.

**Funny-Smelly-Sexy.** Smiley face. Don't get laughs by displaying what you're doing to the audience.

**Gibberish.** Must take the action forward. Best only in pure gibberish. Excellent game on a bad night.

**Hat Game.** Practice until it is impossible to take a hat from you. Practice until you can always take a hat. See Improv For Storytellers.

**He Said, She Said.** Smiley face. - Make sure the actors aren't controlling themselves. Don't use long paragraphs - don't describe what already happened.

**I Love You Scene.** Smiley. Wonderful for contrast. Screwed up by improvisers being funny. Blame the judges.

**Invisibility Scene.** Two person endowing invisibility on other actor. Use real props. (Rewrite description.) Don't bump into each other. Think the other person is crazy - not invisible. Advanced game. Beginners shouldn't play.

**Moving Bodies.** Smiley face. Great audience member game. The players being moved are responsible for moving the scene forward. Warn the audience members not to hurt the people. Don't get a suggestion. Always provide furniture.

**Nothing, Scene From.** Smiley face. Most scenes should be scenes from nothing. Go on the stage and start a scene and take it forward.

**One Hit Wonders.** Take it out of the book.

**One Word at a Time Scene.** Word at a time scene is usually two actors telling a story together and acting it out. There are all kinds of variants but this one is really the best. All the variants ought to be listed together with a note that the original game with two people is really better.

**Physical Contact, Speak Only When In.** This is a Spolin game.

**Pivot.** Training game. Keep it short.

**Reverse, Scene in.** Variant - Do the scene forward and then do that same bit in reverse. (With the Theatre Machine in the 50s. A class Keith did where you do the scenes in as many ways as possible.)

**Sideways Scene.** (Our description is a variant) Back wall is used as floor in Keith's version.

**SoundScape.** Often a mike is used. (Keith has an article in Plays and Players - August 1964. Keith's article is called – "Improvisation and all That Jazz")

**Status Tower.** It's quite fun; you can do this with 30 or 40 people.

**Status Transfer.** Keith calls this a Transformation Game; you can also transfer speed. The status transfer is Keith's; the emotional transfer is from Spolin's.

**Stop Action Narrative.** Variant of the typing game.

**Story from the Audience.** Repeat the story even if you think everybody heard it, because it emphasizes your control of the stage. Keith's advice is to put a spin on the story or take it from a different angle.

**Timed scenes.** Play this game rarely. Keith's feeling about time limit scenes: I think they're avoiding one of the essential problems, which is knowing how to develop material on the stage. They're great for a novelty or for a training game.

**Typewriter.** It is important to know all the let-outs.

**Using a Member of the Audience.** Replace "treat them well" with "Treat them benevolently and make them the center of attention at all times". You want members of the audience up because it creates enormous benevolence. The audience member is seen as a representative of the audience. If you invite people up when things aren't going well, it won't go well with the audience member, but the other thing is that the kind of maladjusted people who are willing to come up on the stage at those times you absolutely don't want them up there. Only get a member of the audience when the show is going really well. Pick volunteers who make eye contact with you. Never select people who are being volunteered by somebody else.

**Verse, Scene in.** Good preparation for this is to read verse in your spare time. Keep a book of Shakespeare's sonnets by the toilet. If it isn't working, people at the side should help provide rhymes. If the scene is bad, end it quickly. Don't play it safe, say the first line with no idea of what the line is.

**Without the Letter "Blank", Scene.** This game is called the **No 'S' Game!!!!** Don't ask the audience for a letter – (Change the description to: "Use the commonest letters: S, R or T.) The purpose of the game is not to show how clever the players are, it is to stop them thinking ahead."

**X word Scene.** The game 'Three Word Sentences' was invented to keep the actors

from thinking ahead. "X Word Scene" and "N Word Scene" are the same game "People have complexed it up".

**Yes...Sounds good to me...I'll go along with that.** You don't have to write the lines down. A wonderful game for beginners. Four sentences are good.

**Long Form. Guest Game, The** The difficulty getting there. You're trapped in the house with a family you haven't met before. If the guest makes jokes, everything dies. If the family makes untruthful jokes, everything dies. Every family member who is met we need to find out their relationship to the missing family member/friend. Age is important. Players should be listening intently to see what kind of family it is. Watch to see what is developed. All scenes should be kept short. The form is based on short scenes. If family members won't get off, other members can go on and get them off. Sustain the scene for up to 25 minutes or more. Don't allow any scene to expand unless it has great value.

# A Word about Suggestions...

"No one believes me when I say this: 'Don't get suggestions' - it is much more of a risk to do scenes without suggestions. The audience wants to know about you; we learn much more about you if you come out on stage and set up a scene without getting piles of stupid suggestions from the audience. Intelligent audience members know you're improvising and they don't want to see scenes based on stupid suggestions any-way."

—Keith Johnstone

# Playbook Glossary

**Endowment or Endow:** This is the way one player indicates an action, character trait or other information to another player WITHOUT saying it explicitly. For example, if I want to endow you with being a dentist, I might hold my hand to the side of my face, look pained and speak as if my mouth were full of cotton, "Boy am I glad to see you, can you see me now?" If I've done this well, you will know that I want you to play a dentist…if not you might say, 'you've been looking for me, the tooth fairy?', in which case I'd play along with that offer.

Endowment scenes or games often have one or more players isolated (go into a soundproof booth), the rest of the team gets secret information from the audience, and when the player(s) reenter, the team tries to share that information with them during the scene without coming out and telling them, thus "endowing" them with the information. The audience applauds a correct endowment. This information is usually activities or attributes, but almost anything is possible. Usually performed with a time limit, the scenes are fast-paced and high-energy. The teammates do not "show" the player what to do, nor do they play charades or hint or manipulate . . . at least not at first. Create new games with or without time limits and with or without gibberish. See: **Chain Murder, Five Things, Hidden Word En-vironment, Murder Endowment, Secret Endowment, Secret Word Endowment, Environment Endowment, and Expert Endowments**

**Filler:** Any type of game or challenge that does not promote story telling. Freeze Tag is an anti-narrative game. Filler games are good for variety.

GLOSSARY     THE PLAYBOOK     *101*

**Freeze:** A theatrical term meaning to hold perfectly still…as if in a freeze frame of a video.

**Gibberish:** Meaningless sounds created by the players to imitate and take the place of actual language, either English or other languages.

**Hoop:** A game or challenge with a particularly specific and 'gamey' requirement. To fulfill the requirements of the game is like 'jumping through hoops'.

**Jump:** When there is a shift of time or location. **Player:** An improviser performing in a show. Offer: Anything an actor does or says on stage.

**Side Coach:** When an off-stage player or director gives directions to the player during a scene.

**Soundproof booth:** For those times when one player shouldn't hear what the others onstage are saying, players create a virtual soundproof booth with themselves as the walls. Players surround that person, who has plugged his/her own ears, and stand towards the back of the stage and make light-hearted distracting sounds and movements.

**Space Object:** A 'space object' is a pretend object. Since improv uses very few actual props, the players mime the objects in scenes.

**Stage:**

> **Downstage:** The part of the stage closest to the audience.
> **Upstage:** The part of the stage farthest away from the audience.
> **Stage Right:** Imagine you are an actor standing on stage facing the audience. Your right is Stage Right
> **Stage Left:** …and your left is Stage Left.

**Status:** The phrase we use to describe the power dynamics between characters. See *Impro*.

**Tableau:** A visually dramatic scene without movement. As if a picture or collection of statues.

**Technical Zero Games:** A type of game where any score hinges on fulfilling the requirements of the game. If the requirements are not fulfilled, the team gets a zero score.

**Timed Scenes:** Broad definition of any scene that has a specified time limit. Timed scenes are not limited to measurements of the clock (1 Minute Scene, 90 Second Scene, etc.); the time limit can be the length of time of an activity (i.e., Scene In the Time It Takes A Match To Burn Out, or Scene With A Teammate's Head In Bucket of Water, or Scene In The Length Of Time It Takes To Go Next Door and Get a Cheeseburger, that sort of thing. Fairy Tale in a Minute, the Show Tonight in 1 minute.

**Tossup Games:** At times during Theatresports™ matches, it is necessary to have a "winner" quickly and decisively determined. Reasons for this are varied: to determine who plays first, to break a tie, or just a way to vary the entertainment for the evening. There are many games that can be used as a Toss-up. Also, playing "Rock/ Paper/Scissors" (a.k.a. Rochambeau), holding your breath for the longest time and flipping a coin are valid (and useful) possibilities.

# A Few Long Form Formats

There are many different long form improv structures. I've described a few of them in brief. For our purposes I will say that long form improv is a group of theatrical structures that ties a performance together either narratively or the-matically. If you are interested in learning more about long form there are plenty of sources available but this will give you an idea of what's possible.

**Single Genre Improv.** This style of improv is based on a full-length play. Some examples include: Improvised Shakespeare, Murder Mystery, Soap Opera, Horror and Western.

**Multiple Genre/Story Long Form.** These formats jump between different stories or genres. Here are a couple of examples I am familiar with and enjoy: Double Feature™ (developed by Rafe Chase) involves two contrasting stories unfolding simultaneously by 4 actors; Triptych jumps between three different stories three times and often concludes with connecting the stories in some way during the last scenes.

**Harold** The Harold is a living, breathing form and no two Harolds are alike...in many ways, to define it does it an injustice. That said:

**A Harold** is a series of scenes based on one theme, from an audience suggestion. The theme may come from asking the audience to fill in the blank in a question. For example "Why do I always _____?" or "The world would be a better place if _____."

A Harold has three parts, the opening, the middle and the

closing. The opening uses different techniques to reveal different connections to the theme. The middle explores some of the connections discovered in the opening. The closing wraps up the themes.

**The Harold Opening:** In one popular Harold opening all the players move around the stage randomly. One players claps his/her hands, all the players freeze while he/she says a word, phrase, line of dialogue, noise, song or movement inspired by the theme. When he/she is finished the players resume moving until another players claps and the pattern repeats. This is known as "Radar Walk" or "Stop and Go". This continues until the word, phrase, line of dialogue, noise, song or movement inspires a longer scene. Scenes continue and end inspired by the material surfaced by the opening. Transitions between scenes can happen in lots of different ways. One popular transition is to have two actors enter the stage and start their new scene, which effectively interrupts and stops the previous scene.

**A Structured Harold** follows a set structure. The middle section is made up of 3 different stories each story consisting of 3 scenes or acts. The players may be in different stories but they play different characters. Between the set of scene the players present a game that also explores the theme. For example: Story A Act 1, followed by Story B, Act 1, followed by Story C Act 1, followed by a game. The pattern repeats, Story A Act 2, Story B Act 2 Story C Act 2 followed by a game. After the 3rd and final patters there is a closing scene, game or other closing.

*(Del Close created the Harold while working with The Committee in San Francisco and Second City in Chicago.)*

**Harold Variations:** The Harold is a challenging form to write about because it offers the improviser so much freedom. The things that seem constant are that no two Harolds are alike and a Harold lets the audience do some of the work (as opposed to making all the connections for them). If the theme is spirit, the player may create a scene with no obvious connection to spirit, which allows the audience to make their own personal connection. This allows them to participate in the Harold in an active way. **Armando.** This format starts with a monologue (or rant), often from a non-player. After the monologue the players create scenes inspired by the monologue/rant. The monologist may return for more installments of the monologue. The format was named after Armando Diaz from Chicago. The format was created by and named for Armando Diaz from Chicago

**Spontaneous Broadway.** The show is a fictional "backers' audition" for a new Broadway musical. As they enter audience members are asked to write down suggestions for made-up song titles and told that they are playing the role of Broadway "Angels" or financial supporters.

As the show begins, the "Producer" lets the audience know that tonight (s)he will be showing numbers from many musicals and let them decide which one to back. The performers take these suggestions and improvise new Broadway musical numbers on the spot, including show descriptions of the fictional musical, which the song is ostensibly from. At the end of the act the audience fills out blank checks provided for them with the title of the musical they wish to back.

In the second act, the cast presents a full-length musical based on the audience's favorite number. In its pure form the only planning done at intermission is to review what was said in the song set-up and choose a location to start in.

*(Created by Kat Koppett in association with Freestyle Repertory Theatre Company in New York City)*

**The Life Game©**. An volunteer is brought to the stage and interviewed about his/her life. The actors use the material to create scenes. There is an interviewer, a director, several actors, a Scenographer to help with props and a musician. The interviewer asks the guest questions about their life and every 3 minutes (or so) the director stages a scene exploring the material revealed. After every scene the guest is asked if that was the way it was.

The form is about honoring the guest in every way so that they continue to open up and tell us more about their life and experiences. If the actors take too much liberty with the material it may be funny but the guest will withdraw and if the players treat it too seriously it may become therapeutic or cathartic. At the end of a successful evening of the Life Game© the audience leaves the theatre talking not about the performances but about their own lives. *The Life Game© was created by Keith Johnstone (see licensing information visit wwwkeithjohnstone.com).*

**Triple Play** jumps between three different genre stories (often a Play, a Movie & a Musical). Each story is alternately played out in three acts. The stories do not blend or mix. This format is often directed. *(Developed by Forest Brakeman and Impro Theater in Los Angles, CA)*

**Guest Game, The You** arrive at a house to visit your boy/girlfriend for the weekend, after having had great hardship getting there. The weather's awful. You can't leave . . .all the buses have stopped running and there is no taxi. Somebody lets you (the Guest) in and your arrival is unexpected. The family member identifies her/himself and finds a reason to leave. You need solid information about this first family member. Let the guest wait a while. The audience likes the guest the more they suffer with her/him. Bring in other people from the household, as in a rush hour, coming and going. Guests keep asking where the friend is. Start reincorporating, playing longer scenes with fewer people. Don't resolve situations too soon. Try to avoid gags! The guest represents the audience. Don't introduce too many ideas. Think about families you know. *(Developed by Keith Johnstone)* (K*)

**More or Less.** One person starts to direct an entire improvised 'play', after a scene or two the action stops and the audience is asked if they want to see 'more' (continue) or 'less' (give another director a chance at a new 'play'). This pattern continues every few scenes. *(Developed by the Loose Moose Theatre Company in Calgary, Alberta, Canada)*

**Super Scene** (AKA Director's Cut) This is a directed elimination improv format. Directed elimination improv format. Four or more directors are introduced. Each director declares the kind of story he or she will tell (for example, "I will tell an epic story of adventure and action.") The directors will perform in each other's scene and there may be additional actors in the cast. Each director directs Scene 1 of his or her story, which often ends with a cliffhanger.

Directors stand in a row before the audience and tease them with what might happen in the next scene. The audience applauds for each scene. The director with the least amount of applause is eliminated. The eliminated director, however, will continue to act in the other scenes.

The remaining directors, direct Scene 2 of their stories. And one is eliminated using the process above.

This continues until the only one director and one story remain and this is the final scene: the Super Scene.

*(I learned Super Scene from Rod Ben Zeev in Amsterdam who told me it originated from Edmonton-but I can't find an Edmonton source. )*

# A Few Thoughts on Improv
# and Performing
# How Theatresports™ Began

The story of Keith Johnstone's inspiration in creating Theatresports™ is folklore among Theatresports™ players: "Johnstone envied the enthusiasm of sports crowds which were always lively and totally engaged in the action". I interviewed Keith and was delighted to learn more about the invention of Theatresports™. He verified his 'sports crowd envy' and added that whenever Theatresports™ needs adjustment - he refers back to Professional Wrestling.

In London in the late 50's Johnstone was using improvisation to teach acting. He and his contemporaries began exploring the idea of using competition to teach improvisation. "It seems totally obvious now, doesn't it?" asked Johnstone, "To have teams compete and see who is best at not negating ideas, it seems obvious now. But it wasn't obvious then.

I was surprised to learn that in England in the 50's, censorship laws were so strict that no public improvisation was allowed. Censorship was so thorough that gestures could not be made on stage that had not been approved, prior to performance, by appointees of the Crown.

So when Keith first conceived of Theatresports™, he couldn't pursue it due to censorship laws. It was twenty years before the first public performance of Theatresports™ in Calgary in 1977, today the international network of Theatresports™ has spread to 23 countries. Not only do teams get together to play but also to exchange ideas, theories, and new formats. BATS Improv has been proud to be part of that network since 1986.

*-Rebecca Stockley, Former Dean of BATS Improv San Francisco*

# What is Risk?

**A Conversation between Keith Johnstone and Rebecca Stockley**

**Keith:**  I hate that four-way dubbing scene! It is never any good and there is never any story!

**Rebecca:**  I've seen it with a story

**Keith:** You have? What was it?

**Rebecca:** I, er, don't, um, remember - but...

**Keith:** Ah HAH!

**Rebecca:**  But I'm sure I've seen it work, we do it a lot here and we're good at it.

**Keith:**  Why do you do it?

**Rebecca:**  It's risky.

**Keith:**  That isn't risk! A solo scene is a risk - a hat game is a risk - there is no risk in that. The problem is that you people misunderstand risk.

**Rebecca:**  We do four-way dubbing a lot.

**Keith:**  Well you shouldn't, it's awful. That speaking in order is bad too - I'm afraid I'm to blame for that one, I invented it for a TV show and now I wish I hadn't. Standing-sitting-lying is good, though, but that one isn't mine, you know.

# The 'Go-To-List'
# from Dennis Cahill

Dennis Cahill, the Associate Artistic Director of Loose Moose Theatre, sent me this list of 'go-to' games.  They are of value to the improvisor to perform over and over as well as fun for the audience to see over and over.

Arms
He Said, She Said
Typewriter
Dubbing (One on One)
Gibberish
Hat Game
Mantra Games
Scene Without "S"
Speaking in One Voice Story in One Voice
Word at a Time Scene (also called Mutants)

Some 'Anti-Narrative' Games:

Chain Murder
Emotional Lists
Growing & Shrinking Machine
Scene in Reverse

# William's Note Book

A few notes and favorite quotes.

"The game is to be altered in front of a bunch of people staring at you." *–Keith Johnstone*

"Answer the questions in the minds of the audience and answer it in the way they (the audience) want it to be answered. You can add plenty to it if you satisfy the basic stuff that the audience wants dealt with." *—Keith Johnstone*

"It is not enough to accept ideas, you must provoke ideas that force things to tilt and change."          *—Keith Johnstone*

"Most scenes are a little too entertaining for me; we're looking for more truth."          *—Keith Johnstone*

"Ideas are crammed into scenes to keep the material from being developed. Any idea is a good idea if you develop it! A great idea is terrible if you don't need it." *—Keith Johnstone*

"Interest will be held when people are altered by others."
          *—Keith Johnstone*

"Information is a low form of communication."
          *—Viola Spolin*

"Play touches and stimulates vitality, awakening the whole person – mind, body, intelligence and creativity."
          *—Viola Spolin*

"When you are in your head, you are alone on the stage."
—*Viola Spolin*

"You can't chase laughs…they'll just run away. You have to create a place where laughs want to come."
—*Jeff Raz, SF Clown Conservatory Director*

"For an artist the difference between a groove and a rut is very thin."          —*Bill Irwin, Clown, Actor*

"The audience wants to see actors in trouble. Just as in the circus, the audience likes to see the lion tamer stick his head into the lion's mouth, not just make the lion move around the cage."
—*Rebecca Stockley & Linda Belt, "Improvisation through Theatresports"*

"Consistency is alright in minor characters. But heroes should normally go through some journey."
—*Keith Johnstone*

"The more Improv there is, the more improv there is."
—*Rebecca Stockley, Improviser*

# Emcee or Host?

Improv is an actor's medium. Improv requires the actor to be the writer, director and dramaturge. What happens on stage is at the complete discretion of the actor. Yet I often see strong MCs calling the shots; telling the actors when to come on and what type of scenes to do.

I'm told, "The Emcee must warm up the audience, keep the show moving, the audience energized and look after the shape-of-the-show". But the actors could do that.

It might be nice to have someone to greet the audience and make announcements from time to time. This would be more of a host than a ringleader.

We want inspired actors who want to create theatre not obedient well behaved performers jumping when called.

# Lessons from a Life of Improv

An interview with Randy Dixon of Unexpected Productions of Seattle, Washington.

Randy Dixon was 15 years old when he took an improv class because his friend didn't want to attend alone. We talked about his early days in improv: the joys, the dangers, the games and the formats.

**How did Theatresports™ get to Seattle?**

The connection actually came from Del Close. I was taking classes from Second City alum Roberta McGuire. During a trip to Chicago Roberta talked with Del Close, who had just finished reading Impro and recommended that Roberta contact this guy Keith Johnstone. So Keith came to Seattle in 1982 and taught a Theatresports™ workshop. By 1983 there were regular Monday night Theatresports™ performances.

**How did it work in the beginning?**

It was like Bowling Night, nobody really took it seriously. We were all in these other groups but for a laugh we'd get together on Monday nights and play Theatresports™ and we could work with different people. Teams would break up and reform all the time.

**How did it become serious?**

We found that the people who were really competitive had to leave. It was always hard when people really wanted to win. At first people were really attracted to the competition aspect of it but then it got in the way and people started to be unkind. But most people didn't take it too seriously.

**Did you have an audience?**

No. Often there were fewer people in the audience than on stage. That helped us to keep it about having fun and the work.

**Were you just a Theatresports™ shop?**

Yes. But we wanted to do other project too. Most of the people involved at that time were actors, improvisers and sketch comedians from other groups. In Seattle we started in Long Form first then found the games.

**How would you characterize those early days?**

Well one of our committee members had a 4 year old daughter who walked out during one of the meetings saying, 'Theatresports, Theatresports, talk, talk, talk'. We were all arguing and she stopped it right then.

**Who was in charge?**

Membership. We'd get into these huge fights and we'd argue and cry and there were threats of fist fights. And finally in 1985 or 86 we voted to go to **Improv Lessons** a more traditional structure with an Artistic Director and that sort of thing. So the membership basically voted itself out of power. We began to elect people to be the Artistic Director and management.

**What makes Theatresports™ as a format so attractive?**

You can almost do anything. There is nothing in the rules that say you can't. It's flexible enough to hold anything you want to throw at it. Primarily this tends to be short form games. There are so many games and such an eclectic taste in the improv community it really allows for everybody to do a little bit of everything they want to do. From an audience point of view, it's pretty straightforward. People get sports. When I describe a Harold to somebody they say "What? Why would I want to see that?" When they see it they say, "that's great." But Theatresports™ it's pretty straightforward. You just have to talk about sports and everybody gets sports. As soon as you talk about it, the audience goes, okay, it is something I can sink my teeth into, I won't be completely in the dark. Going to watch the show I'll have something I can watch and understand.

### What would you say to someone just starting out in Theatresports™?

As soon as you introduce Theatresports™ you bring in that competitive aspect. It's really important at the beginning to lay down the philosophy of what you want the competition to be or not be. I am sure there are people who would want it to be cut throat competitive, and that's fine too but lay down those ground rules from the very beginning. It's difficult to introduce the sporting aspect, the competitive aspect and then try to explain that it's not competitive. Which sort of happened to us. We realized that some people were having problems with each other and there was a lot of competition going on. It wasn't healthy.

### What is your advice about issuing challenges?

It's about the show. What I hope is that, people will watch the stage and ask, what does the show need? And take care of each other. So if you're playing against a team that is having a rough night, issue a challenge to help get them back on their feet. When we watch out for each other then the show is going to be good. When you're having a really good night take more chances.

What I often see is that people having a great show whip out the same five games they always play rather than rising to the occasion. If a show is really tanking by all means play games that are strong for your team.

For me, improv is about variety, the only way you can do that is to have a knowledge of the games. I encourage people to get to know as many games as you can so that when you have a certain situation on stage you're not left with the same 3 things you always do.

## How do games release creativity?

Imagine falling through blackness, it's terrifying. When am I going to land? Where am I? But if you have anything to hold on to, even a point in the distance giving you perspective it makes you feel safer. That's what many of the games do it gives you something to hold on to. If you focus on the rules of the game than you can bypass the internal editor then creativity is allowed to flow freely. But you need that one little thing to hold on to.

## What is the Keith Johnstone rule about games?

Keith said that if you give any improviser a game the first impulses will be to change the rules. And that any rule change that an improviser makes to a game makes the game safer to play.

I think he's right. I've seen improvisers change the rules of a game even before they play the game, rather than try it and see if it works.

# Starting Your Own Improv Group.

I used to teach a two-day workshop on how to start your own improv group. I would focus on mission statements, negotiations with venue owners, how to recruit players, and how to build ensemble. Then it occurred to me that I could teach the entire subject matter much more effectively with only four words.

Those four words are: First Make the Flyer.

In making the flyer you will be required to answer all the questions necessary to put a group together. You'll have to list the location, time, group name, format, cast and admission price. And the graphics you choose will reveal your group identity.

The next challenge for a new improv group comes after the first few shows. You will reach a point where you've done it...now what? That's when the internal power struggles may begin and to get through that, you'll need both wise leadership and a clear purpose.

Good luck, William Hall

# Goals of an improv group:

1. the stage is a safe place

2. the work is worthwhile

3. fill all the seats

4. have repeat audience

*—Keith Johnstone*

# My Improv Bookshelf

There are many, many books on improvisation; these are some of my favorites:

**Impro: Improvisation and the Theatre** by Keith Johnstone Routledge/Theatre Arts Books ISBN 0-87830-117-8

**Impro for Storytellers** by Keith Johnstone Routledge/Theatre Arts Books ISBN 0-87830-105-4

**"Don't be Prepared" Theatresports™ for Teachers** by Keith Johnstone —OUT OF PRINT- ISBN 0-98698382-0-4

**Free Play** by Stephen Nachmanovich Jeremy P. Tarcher, Inc. ISBN 0-87477-578-1

**Truth in Comedy: The Manual for Improvisation** by Charna Halpern, Del Close & Kim "Howard" Johnson Meriwether Publishing Ltd. ISBN 1-56608-003-7

**Something Wonderful Right Away** edited by Jeffrey Sweet Avon Books ISBN 0-380-01884-5

**"*Emphasis on Sport*" in Brecht on Theatre** by Bertolt Brecht translation by John Wilett Hill and Wang ISBN 8090-0542

**Improv Wisdom** by Patricia Ryan Madson Bell Tower ISBN 1400081882

**Improvisation Through Theatresports**
by Lynda Belt & Rebecca Stockley
Thespis Productions
— Soon to be republished Impro:
   Improvisation and the Theatre

**Improvisation For The Theater: a Handbook of
Teaching and Directing Techniques** by Viola Spolin
Northwestern University ISBN 0-8101-0018-5

**Theatresports Down Under** by Lyn Pierse
Improcorp Australia Pty Ltd. Kensington NSW, Australia
ISBN 0-646-13286-5

**Zen in the Art of Archery** by Eugen Herrigel
Vintage Books (A Division of random House, Inc.)
ISBN 0-679-72297-1

**Training To Imagine: Practical Improvisational
Theatre Techniques to Enhance Creativity, Teamwork,
Leadership and Learning** by Kat Koppett
Stylus Publishing ISBN 1-57922-033-9

**Games for Actors and Non-Actors**
by Augusto Boal
Routledge ISBN 0-415-26708-0

**Improvisation in Drama (New Directions in Theatre)**
by Anthony Frost and Ralph Yarrow
Palgrave Macmillan  ISBN 0-311-04746-0

# The Source of Games

Most of these games came to me through other Theatresports™ leagues in the late 1980s when we got started (Seattle, Vancouver & Edmonton). Since then many people have contributed games. Someone would see a game played somewhere else and tell me about it or our group would develop one. Many of the games can be traced to Viola Spolin (with Neva Boyd) and Keith Johnstone either directly or indirectly.

I've come to understand that most games have a theory behind them; for example, Touch Talk, (talking only when in physical contact with another player) pushes the performers to pay attention and interact with each other. Yes, it's true; some improvisers don't look at each other while on stage creating a scene. If you want to invent a new game, look for a theory and explore it with a game.

If you know of a game that isn't in this collection, please send it in so we can share it with the rest of the improv community.

—*WilliamHall*, william@fratellibologna.com

# Improv on the web:

There are many many great sites for improvisation on the internet.

Here are a few of my favorite:

> www.theatresports.org
> www.theatresports.com
> www.appliedimprov.net
> www.keithjohnstone.com
> ~~www.ImprovPlaybook.com~~
> www.ImprovGames.com
> www.ImprovNotebook.com

# Free Improv

During an evening of Theatresports™, a host/director leads the improvisers through some basic exercises for the audience.

Then primary reason for doing this is to educate the audience about what they are about to see. An educated audience will enjoy the performances more and will be interested in taking classes. It can also be a way to get other improvisers a little stage time.

Some of the games used are: Offer/Block, Offer/Accept; Hat Game; Making Faces (The King Game); The Knee Game; "I Love You" Mantra. The evening's Emcee can serve as host/director or another experienced improviser can do the job.

# Grateful Acknowledgments

When I was younger I never understood why actors accepting awards would thank so many people. Working on this book has made it clear to me. There are no solo achievements. There are so many people who have made this book possible. They all are a living testimony to the creative and generous spirit of the arts and improvisational theatre.

I am deeply grateful to **Keith Johnstone** and **Rebecca Stockley** for opening up so many doors to the creative community and a life of exploration.

**Paul Killam** worked enthusiastically on the earlier versions of this playbook and I am deeply grateful to his passion and work. Thank you **BATS Improv** community for their generosity, support and study of improv.

**Ann Feehan** worked as my assistant editor for several months organizing this book. Her pragmatic approach and gleeful enthusiasm over the games helped sustain me through the project.

Thanks to **John X. Heart** for the playful cartoons. Thanks to **Randy Dixon** for the interview and ongoing conversation about this still emerging art form. Thank you to **Jay Alexander** and **Keith Moreau** for helping me learn a new computer program.

Thank you to **Patricia Pearson** for her layout tips. Thanks **Joshua Raoul Brody** for his keen eye for spelling, grammar and common sense.

I am thankful for my partner in life **Carla Hatley**, who supports and celebrates life in so many ways. She reminds me that a walk with the dog is often more important than an hour on the computer.

I want to thank everyone who plays improv. It is a passionate and giving community. **Jim Cranna** (The Committee) once told me, "'yes and' answers any question about improv". That may be true for the improv community as well.

And for their support and contributions I'd like to thank:

| | |
|---|---|
| Barbara Scott | Fuzzy Gerdes |
| Tara McDonough | Patricia Ryan Madson |
| Terry Sandke | Chet Anderson |
| Rich Cox | The Living Playbook |
| Lisa Rowland | Dave Bushnell |
| Zoe Galvez | Freddy HahneThe Human |
| Ed Alter | Ping Pong |
| Dave Dyson | Rafe Chase |
| John Remak | Dennis Cahill |
| Chris Sams | Ball Site |
| Christian Utzman | Scott J. Miller |
| Stephen Kearin | Teresa Roberts |
| David Norfleet | Ward Miller |
| Kimberly MacLean | Sean Hill |
| James Faulkner | Jenny Meyers Rosen |
| Dave Bushnell | Tom Coates |
| Jason Leal | |

# Alphabetical Index of Games

Your Personal Notes,
Doodles and New Games

Your Personal Notes,
Doodles and New Games

Your Personal Notes,
Doodles and New Games

Your Personal Notes,
Doodles and New Games

Your Personal Notes,
Doodles and New Games

Your Personal Notes,
Doodles and New Games

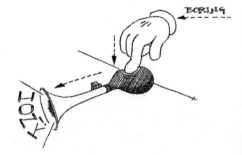

# Order More Playbooks

## Give the Gift of Improv

Imagine your friends' faces when they receive a book filled with improv games from you as a gift.

Order a box for your group.

Contact William Hall
www.ImprovPlaybook.com
www.ImprovGames.com
or www.FratelliBologna.com

# Licensing

Theatresports™ is a registered as a trademark and been copyrighted. This means that, similar to main-stage productions such as "Les Misérables", you need to have permission to use the format.

Keith Johnstone, creator of the improvisational shows Theatresports™, Maestro Theatre™, and Gorilla Theater™, founded the International Theatresports™ Institute (ITI) in 1998 to manage the international rights to these show formats. If you wish to preform or teach them, you need to obtain permission in the form of a performance rights agreement from the ITI.

It's easy to apply. Find FAQs and download the form online here:
http://theatresports.com/how-to-apply/

For the Life Game© and Keith Johnstone Workshops
www.KeithJohnstone.com • workshops@keithjohnstone.com

# About the Editor
## William Hall

William is an actor, director, trainer and mask maker.
In 1986, his friend Rebecca Stockley said, "I've written a cool story, guess what it's about?" After about ten minutes William had guessed the whole story. When she revealed that he had written the story with his guesses, William's life changed. He realized that there were stories in all of us and that storytelling could be effortless.

He worked with a few brave folks in San Francisco and started BATS Improv. Today BATS Improv is a thriving improv community with a 200-seat theatre, a full-time staff and a spirit of growth and exploration that make it a great place for actors, students and audiences.

He's performed and taught improv all over the world and even directed The Life Game© in Lodz, Poland. He has been in a few movies, TV shows and commercials.

His company, Fratelli Bologna, designs and delivers training for theater groups and corporations. Using the principles and theories of improvisation, Fratelli Bologna works with companies and individuals to increase engagement and authentic leadership.
— William Hall

playbook@fratellibologna.com
www.fratellibologna.com

Made in the USA
San Bernardino, CA
20 March 2016